DISCOVERING
THE SEA

DISCOVERING
THE SEA
by Sandra Smith

Published by

STONEHENGE

in association with

The American Museum of Natural History

The author
Dr Sandra Smith is chairman of the Oceanography course at the
British Open University. A Cambridge graduate in geology, she
spent five years doing marine research in the Department of
Geodesy and Geophysics at Cambridge, where she obtained her
PhD. She has taken part in many research cruises, particularly in
the eastern Mediterranean, and has started working in the Pacific
Ocean with the Scripps Institution of Oceanography, La Jolla,
California. The Smith Seamount in the Pacific has been named for
Dr Smith. Sailing a 34-foot boat in the North Sea is her relaxation.

The consultants
Sir George Deacon, CBE, DSc, is a Fellow of the Royal Society and
former Director of Britain's National Institute of Oceanography.
He worked for over ten years aboard the research ships *William
Scoresby* and *Discovery II*, and has been President of the Royal
Institute of Navigation. He holds the Alexander Agassiz Medal of
the US National Academy of Sciences, the Polar Medal and a
number of other international distinctions and awards.

Dr David A. Ross, who took his doctoral studies at Scripps
Institution of Oceanography on the Pacific coast of California, is
now Senior Scientist at the Woods Hole Oceanographic Institution
on the Atlantic coastline of Massachusetts. His research specialities
are in marine geology and geophysics, with particular emphasis
on cooperative research programs with other nations, in the
Mediterranean and elsewhere. The author of more than 100
publications and editor or author of nine books, he has also served
on the ocean affairs advisory committee for the US Department of
State.

Stonehenge Press Inc.:
Publisher: John Canova
Editor: Ezra Bowen
Deputy Editor: Carolyn Tasker

Trewin Copplestone Books Ltd.:
Editorial Director: James Clark
Managing Editor: Barbara Horn
Title Editor: Hugh Morgan

Created, designed and produced by
Trewin Copplestone Books Ltd, London.

Library of Congress catalogue card number 81-50814
Printed in U.S.A. by Rand McNally & Co.
First printing
ISBN 0-86706-000-x

Set in Monophoto Rockwell Light by
SX Composing Ltd, Rayleigh, Essex, England
Separation by Scan Studios Ltd, Dublin, Ireland

Contents

The World of the Sea

Some people live near the sea and others spend much of their lives at sea, but many millions more have never seen the sea even once in their lives. So although we all know the sea is there, it is probably true to say that most of us have very little idea of how much there is to learn about it, whether we look at it as a source of necessities, such as food and fuel, as the home of an almost incredible variety of life forms, or as the setting for the whole epic of seamanship; or, in possibly the least familiar way, as a kind of history book made of rocks and fossils that tells us how long ago the continents were formed and how far they have moved over the face of the earth.

On a map or globe the sea may look like an unvarying expanse of blue that covers more of the surface than the land does. Seen from our shores, it may stretch away as a gray or green emptiness. Yet underneath that seemingly monotonous surface there is another world, one that is in many respects not too different from the one we live in. We have climates, plant life, major features of the surface. So does the sea. It has events such as landslips, earthquakes, sinkages, eruptions and erosions, just as we do on land.

We would, of course, know the sea better if we could see into it more easily. We see its inhabitants when they are fished out as food, and a number of them are kept for us to look at in aquariums and zoos. But to try to see their own environment as they know it themselves requires quite an effort of our imaginations. The meaning of density, salinity, temperature and flow in the seawater is for them a matter of life or death. Elaborate chains of life at different biological levels are the basis of their food resources – one set of creatures feeding on smaller ones all the way down the line. Such chains have to be kept intact, as any breakdown could spell disaster for one or more species somewhere in it. This complicated balance of plant and animal life is not merely a matter for them of keeping alive, but concerns the solid foundations of the earth itself. As they die, the remains of microscopic animals and plants rain down and form beds of rock at the bottom of the sea. They have been doing so since the dawn of life on earth and are still doing so. The layers they have formed have, in the course of time, come to be thrust up in the form of mountain ranges towering above the surface and bearing fossil sea shells in the rocks at their summits.

Facts like these open up another view, which looks at the sea not only as a living world parallel to our own but also as a perpetually shifting scene. The seawater, framed between the bottom and the coast, is not passive and quiet. It is being changed all the time by changes in the amount of ice locked up at the Poles, the cycle of rainfall and evaporation, and the slow creation of new rocks welling up from the interior of the earth. In one way or another, all of this has been going on since a crust first began to form on a fiery earth. The sea floors have never settled down. Mountains are always being made, destroyed and remade. Oceans have opened and closed over hundreds and millions of years, leaving their mark in the tangled layers of rock that we see on land.

The scale of facts concerning the sea may seem daunting, such as the existence of mountains higher than Mount Everest and of chasms seven miles deep. Its floods and hurricanes are frightening. Its extent tempts us to think of it as unending. We may prefer not to think about these aspects of the sea, looking on it instead as a provider of food, as a way for ships, as a yielder of minerals and fuel.

We are living in a very good time in which to satisfy curiosity about the sea. With new techniques scientists are probing not only the deepest sea floor, but what lies below it. With satellite photography from space and sophisticated earthquake studies, they are mapping the movements of the currents and the continents in ways that were impossible a short time ago. This book is designed to present this fascinating new knowledge directly and clearly.

Earth and Its Oceans

Photographs of the earth taken from lunar space missions show it as a beautiful blue and white ball. The blue is the ocean and the white swirls are the clouds. The only planet in the solar system to have oceans, the earth appears mainly blue because water covers more of its surface than do the continents – seventy-one per cent or almost three-quarters. This water is not distributed evenly over the earth's surface. Most of the land lies in the northern hemisphere, while most of the southern hemisphere is ocean, with a continuous belt of water linking the three major oceans.

The earth's three major oceans are the Pacific, the Atlantic, and the Indian Oceans. The Pacific, which is the largest, covers sixty-four million square miles – about the same size as the Atlantic and the Indian Oceans combined. It covers more than a third of the surface of the earth and stretches almost half way around it from east to west. It is so large that all the land on the earth's surface could fit within its borders. The Atlantic Ocean is next in size and although it stretches as far north and south as the Pacific, it is narrower and has an irregular shape, being 4500 miles across at its widest point, compared with 12,500 miles in the Pacific. The Indian Ocean is the smallest of the major oceans, and is roughly triangular in shape. The Arctic is much smaller than the major three and is covered almost entirely with ice.

The earth also has smaller water-covered areas called seas, such as the Mediterranean and the Caribbean. Seas may be part of an ocean – the Caribbean, for example, is part of the Atlantic – or they may be separate, like the Mediterranean.

Compared with the diameter of the earth, the depth of its oceans is minute. Even the deepest part, which is in the western Pacific, descends only seven miles, while the earth's diameter is about 8000 miles. On a model of the earth the size of an orange, the depth of the oceans would be about the thickness of a thin layer of paper.

After the Pacific had been explored by Europeans in the sixteenth century, its large size and roughly circular shape made some scientists think that it might have been a hole left when the moon separated from the earth. We now know that the average depth of the Pacific is only about three miles, so that the amount of solid land that could have been scooped out of the whole area would be less than 200 million cubic miles – not nearly enough to form a body the size of the moon, which consists of more than five billion cubic miles!

Earth's thin watery covering is what made life possible on earth. The earliest forms of life developed in the ocean and evolved there before moving to the land. Today, the oceans provide food, water, chemicals, and even power. They moderate our climate by absorbing heat in tropical areas, thereby cooling them, and carrying it to the freezing polar areas, which would otherwise become even colder. We use them as highways between the continents and, unfortunately, as a dumping-ground for waste. Without them, we could not exist.

The oceans and some of the principal seas on an equal-area projection of the earth

An earth-view (left) from Apollo 11 in July 1969 shows how blue the water makes our planet appear in space, unlike the other members of the solar system.

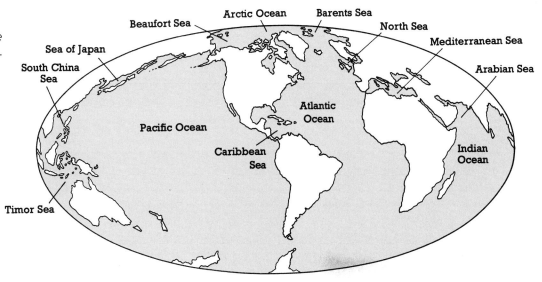

Where the Water Came From

The water on the earth's surface that now fills the oceans got there as part of a process that started with the origin of the earth itself. This is the opinion of most earth-scientists today. To understand that process, we need to know something about the origin of the solar system. The material from which the earth and the other planets were later to be formed probably began as a cloud of gases spinning around the sun. These gases gradually condensed, making solid particles. Many of them collided, and built up larger and larger concentrations of matter.

The part that was eventually to become the earth seems to have cooled and begun solidifying about 4.6 billion years ago, and as the spinning movement shaped matter into a ball, it contracted even further. Under these pressures, matter at the center of the newly formed earth began to heat up again and became molten. When this happened, water that had been contained inside the earth was released to the surface as vapor and was added to the primitive atmosphere. When it cooled and condensed, it fell to the surface as rain and eventually formed the first oceans. We do not know how much of the water in the oceans came from this source. Estimates range from a third to almost all of it – there is no way we can determine the exact amount. Neither can we tell when this happened, but some indication comes from rocks. The oldest rock discovered so far on the earth's surface is from Greenland and is 3.8 billion years old. It is a kind of rock formed from pebbles laid down under water and later compressed. This shows that water must already have condensed and fallen to earth during the 800 million years that had passed since the earth was formed.

The rest of the water in the oceans also came from the interior of the earth, but was forced to the surface by volcanic eruptions and hot springs. There are many volcanoes and hot springs on land and even more in parts of the ocean, and they are still spewing out water. Only a small proportion of this water is new, or juvenile, water coming from deep inside the earth for the first time. Most of it is groundwater or seawater that seeped down into the earth, heated up through contact with hot rocks and then returned to the surface in a volcanic eruption or a hot spring. Although only a small proportion of this water is juvenile, the total amount of new water brought to the surface in the billions of years this process has been going on has been enough to help fill the oceans.

Was the water that came from the earth's interior to fill the oceans the same salty seawater we know today? As far as we can tell, the oceans never had fresh water. Salt, or salinity, comes from gases and other substances dissolved in the water. When water first rose to the surface of the earth as steam, it contained gases, some of which dissolved in the original oceans. Since then, volcanoes have supplied other gases along with water and added them to the oceans. Other substances in seawater reached and still reach the ocean by a different process. They come from rocks on land which slowly break down to produce tiny fragments that flow in rivers into the oceans.

Although the ocean, like the atmosphere, had very little oxygen up to about 1.9 billion years ago and had differing amounts of gases and metals in the past, the total amount of all dissolved substances in the ocean – the salinity – was probably similar to the present. And about 1 billion years ago the oceans reached a composition very similar to what it is today.

Just as substances are being added to seawater, so also are they being removed. If they were not, the concentration would go on building up. Water is still being added to the oceans by volcanoes, rain and rivers, and is being lost again by evaporation. The salinity of seawater remains at the same level because some of the solids sink to the bottom or are thrown into the air in sea spray. Salt particles attract

water in the atmosphere and droplets grow on them, some of which are blown away over the land as rain. By these means, water and solids are recycled through the atmosphere, rivers, sediments, sea-water, rock, and the earth's interior to maintain the overall composition of the oceans.

The plume of steam rising from Boquerón volcano on San Benedicto island, about 350 miles off the Pacific coast of Mexico, adds an almost imperceptible amount of water to the atmosphere, and in turn to the oceans. All volcanoes in the world are contributing to the same process.

Sea-level Changes

Although tides and winds constantly change water levels, the average level of the sea in relation to the land at any place – the mean sea-level – remains the same for many years, long enough to make it a useful reference level on maps. However, sea-level has changed considerably over longer periods. Valleys ground into U-shapes by glaciers on land now lie below sea-level along the spectacular fjord coast-lines of Norway and western Canada. Forests that once grew on land are now submerged around the coast of Britain. The bones and teeth of mammoths, dinosaurs and other animals that once lived on land have been found off the coast of the United States and Europe. All this evidence indicates that sea-level has risen relative to the land.

This rise probably occurred when ice, formed during the last ice age, melted. During an ice age, the polar ice grows and covers a large part of the earth.

Raised beaches on the Scottish Island of Eigg, left high and dry when the land rose. One is now a sloping shelf, while a later, small one lies behind the present sandy beach.

The Antarctic ice in the area of the South Shetland Islands. The weight of their glaciers and ice caps press the landmasses of both Antarctica and Greenland more deeply into the earth's crust than do the ice-free continents.

The lightest green area shows the submerged land off the present Atlantic coast of the USA which, 15,000 years ago, was above sea-level. The darker green area shows where the dry land would end if all the world's ice were to melt.

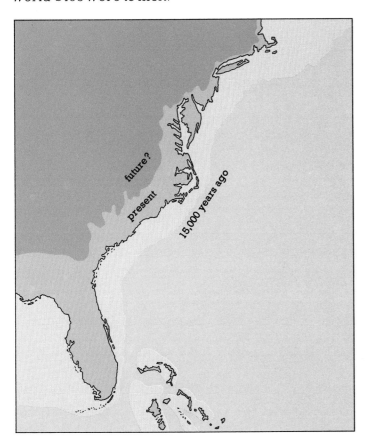

The formation of ice removes water from the oceans and causes the sea-level to fall. When the ice melts, the sea-level rises. The parts of land that are covered with huge sheets of ice during an ice age may also sink under the weight of the ice and rise again when the ice melts. Sometimes the land rises even more than the sea bordering it, forming raised, or uplifted, beaches such as those we see today in Scotland, around the Hudson Bay in Canada, or on the Baltic coast of Scandinavia.

There have been long periods in the past when the earth had little ice. Between the last ice age and the one before it, for example, there was a gap of about 250 million years. The last ice age began more than a million years ago and lasted until about 10,000 years ago, when modern man was already on the scene. It was a time of rapid change in climate, with cold periods, called glacial periods, interspersed with warmer, or interglacial, periods. During the inter-glacial periods, the ice melted, returning water to the oceans and causing sea-level to rise. During the last glacial period, about 15,000 years ago, sea-level was about 400 feet lower than it is now. Between 15,000 and 6000 years ago, sea-level gradually rose at a rate of about half an inch a year. During the last 6000 years or so sea-level has continued to rise, but at the much slower rate of .05 inch per year.

These changes in sea-level affected not only the land but also human life on it. During times of lower sea-level a land bridge now covered by shallow seas linked Asia and North America, and early man and animals may have used this bridge to move from Asia to North and South America. During the rise in sea-level since the last glacial period, people living along coasts or in the lower reaches of rivers had to move inland as the sea advanced.

We do not know at the moment whether the last ice age is over or whether we are still in an interglacial, or warm, period. We do know that the sea-level is still rising very slowly. If all the remaining ice on earth melted, the sea-level would rise by a further 200 feet or so. The eventual effect of such a rise, however slowly it came, would be catastrophic, since a large proportion of the world's population lives near sea coasts. Such a rise in sea-level would drown most of the world's major cities. On the other hand, we could be heading for another glacial period and a falling sea-level. At the moment we cannot tell.

Exploring the Sea Floor

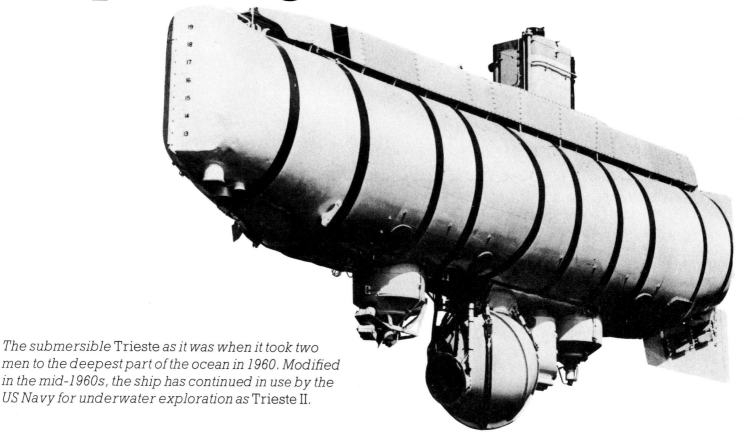

The submersible Trieste *as it was when it took two men to the deepest part of the ocean in 1960. Modified in the mid-1960s, the ship has continued in use by the US Navy for underwater exploration as* Trieste II.

Imagine trying to study the surface of the land from an aircraft flying three miles above it over thick clouds. Scientists trying to learn about the sea floor face similar problems, and for this reason they rely on a range of methods and equipment that help them study the seabed without actually seeing it.

Sound waves can provide oceanographers with "eyes" where light will not reach. The equipment most generally employed is called echo sounding. Sound signals are directed into the water from a moving ship at short intervals. When the signal strikes objects on the bottom, sound waves will be reflected back to instruments in the ship, where the time elapsed between the signal's dispatch and its return is recorded. By calculating the time interval of the sound signal, the depth of the object can be determined to an accuracy of about six feet in three miles of depth, and so a profile of the ocean floor can be built up from a sequence of echo soundings.

Seismic profiling is a kind of echo sounding which uses the more powerful sound waves produced by an explosion – often by releasing compressed air into the water. These sound waves reach below the surface at the bottom of the sea and bounce back off the buried rocks they strike. This gives a profile of geological formations below the surface.

Another device called a side-scan sonar uses sound waves to look at the seabed over a wide area. The sound waves are sent out to the sides and the echo received by a device often called a "fish," towed by the surface vessel. The side-scan sonar was originally developed to find enemy submarines and it produces information about the sea floor that is almost as comprehensive as a photograph. It is also used to locate wrecks and large schools of fish.

Deep-sea cameras can be used to take photographs of the sea floor, but because the bottom of the deep sea is dark, lights must be lowered to the sea bed with the camera. And because light does not penetrate very far in the water, underwater photography and television can be used only for close-ups of small animals or features on the seabed.

Some information about the ocean floor comes from divers who actually go down and look at it. Divers wear bulky diving suits attached to the surface by air lines or they free dive using SCUBA (Self-Contained Underwater Breathing Apparatus). Because the pressure caused by the weight of the water increases as divers descend, however, they cannot safely go down more than about 300 feet wearing SCUBA and 1000 feet or more wearing diving suits, so they can explore only a small part of the total ocean floor.

Humans can, however, explore deeper water in submersibles, small submarine-like vehicles built to withstand the immense pressures in the depths of the oceans. Submersibles usually carry two or three people and are transported by ship to the area of the dive, as they cannot travel long distances. They are slow and expensive, can be launched only when the sea is calm, and can stay down for only a maximum of 72 hours. However, at present they are the only means by which people can actually see most of the ocean floor and they provide a good means for studying it in some respects – collecting rock samples, for example, with appliances controlled from inside the submersible. They can also be used for non-scientific jobs such as laying pipelines, and in 1966 the two submersibles *Alvin* and *Aluminaut* searched for and recovered an atomic bomb lost off the Spanish coast.

In 1960 the submersible *Trieste*, with two men aboard, made a record dive to the deepest part of the oceans, the Challenger Deep in the Pacific, about seven miles down. We had finally reached the deepest part of the ocean only a few years before we made that other great achievement of landing on the moon.

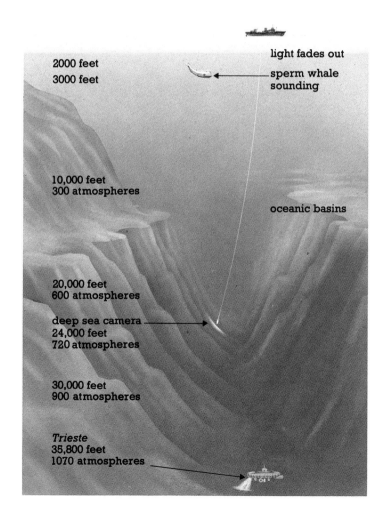

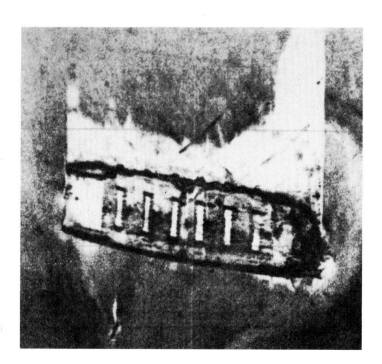

Side-scan sonar is able to produce pictures of objects on the sea floor such as this sunken sailing barge in the Great Lakes.

This simplified diagram of an ocean trench shows water pressures at various depths. One atmosphere equals 14.7 pounds per sq. inch.

Features of the Sea Floor

The discovery that the sea floor is as varied and rugged as the land – and not a flat, empty plain – is one of the most striking that oceanographers have made in the last hundred years.

The earth, we now know, has two main ranges of heights – one above sea-level and one below. Most of the land, which makes up about a quarter of the earth's surface, ranges from sea-level to about a half a mile above sea level. Only about one per cent of the land surface is more than two miles high. Mount Everest, the highest point, rises about five and a half miles. Under the ocean, and covering almost half the earth's surface, the range is from one and a half to three miles below sea-level. Less than one per cent is more than four miles down; the deepest part, the Challenger Deep in the Pacific, is about seven miles below sea-level.

Like the land surface, the seabed has a number of major features, called continental margins, deep ocean floor, ocean ridges, trenches and seamounts. Oceanographers describe these features according to their depth below sea-level, their slope and their general shape. Their position in the ocean in most cases falls into a simpler pattern than the position of features on land.

Continental margins border the land and have three distinct parts. The part closest to land and shallowest, the continental shelf, is generally only a few hundred feet under the water and is relatively flat. At the outer edge of the continental shelf, called the shelf break, the continental slope begins. It descends smoothly down to the continental rise, the outermost part of the continental margin. Beyond the rise is the deep ocean basin. These basins are depressions that cover a large part of the ocean floor. Because they are deep and flat, they are often called abyssal (from abyss) plains.

Rising above the abyssal plains are enormous undersea mountain chains called ocean ridges. The tops of most are between one and two miles below sea-level. A few rise above sea-level; Iceland, for example, is the top of an ocean ridge. Ocean ridges have steep, rough sides and are similar in size and shape to mountain chains on land, but they are much longer. The ridge in the Atlantic Ocean, for example, is longer than the Rocky Mountains, the Andes or the Himalayas. It runs the length of the Atlantic Ocean, and joins a ridge in the Indian Ocean which continues into the Pacific. In some oceans, including the Atlantic and the Indian Oceans, the ridges are central or mid-ocean. They run down the center, dividing the ocean basin roughly into two equal halves. In the Pacific, however, the ridge is closer to the eastern side of the ocean.

Trenches are long, narrow and usually curved. They cut into the seabed and are the deepest part of the ocean. There are few trenches in the Atlantic but they run along the west, north and east sides of the Pacific. Together trenches take up a very small part of the total ocean floor.

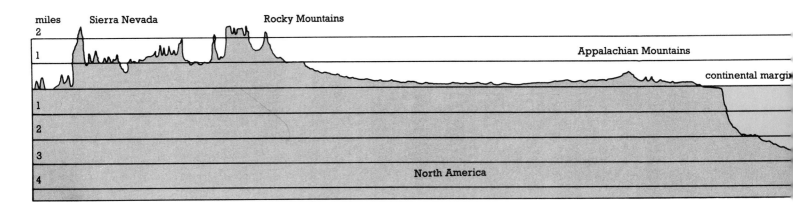

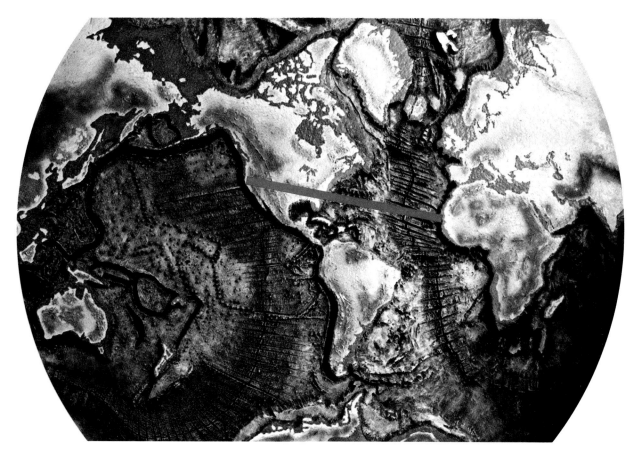

The educational channel of the British Broadcasting Corporation's television service produced the 7 x 4 feet-wide relief model shown above to explain the world's major undersea features to students of earth-sciences. The model shows the continental margins, abyssal plains, mid-ocean ridges, deep trenches, and seamounts. The shallow seas which surround Iceland are, however, not continental margins but are due to material from the mid-ocean ridge. The band drawn across the center marks the profiles of heights and depths shown in the sectional drawing below.

A comparison of the heights of land and ocean floor features on a line running across the USA and the North Atlantic to Africa. In this diagram the heights have been exaggerated in proportion to the width.

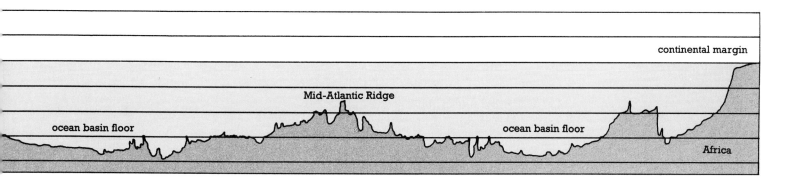

continental margin

Mid-Atlantic Ridge

ocean basin floor

ocean basin floor

Africa

Continental Margins

The best known and most used part of the ocean is the shallow part closest to shore: the continental shelf.

In the past, the continental shelf was defined as the area of ocean from the shore out to the point where the water reached a depth of a hundred fathoms (600 feet). Today we know that water depth varies over the real shelf from about 100 to 1000 feet; and we define the shelf as the area between the shore and the shelf break where the continental slope begins. The depth of the water at the shelf break averages about 400 feet throughout the world, except for heavily glaciated areas like Antarctica and Greenland where it is much deeper, because these land masses are pressed down by the weight of the ice on them.

As its name implies, the continental shelf is relatively flat. It does slope downward, but only about ten feet in a mile. If you were to stand in the middle of the shelf with all the water drained away, you would have a hard time knowing which direction led toward land and which toward the open sea. Standing there, you would find yourself on a layer of sediment. This sediment would look like gravel, sand, or mud

Ripples like these on the sediment of the continental shelf – revealed in this photograph taken twenty feet below the surface of the Caribbean – are created by currents.

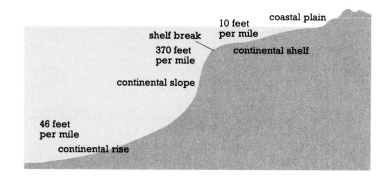

The zones that make up the continental margin: the shelf, *shallow and fairly flat, is next to the coastline;* the shelfbreak *is at about 400 feet of water, where the shelf drops to the* slope; *at the base of the slope lies the* rise, *built up of sediment. Here the ocean floor begins. Some typical gradients are shown.*

North America, the coast of Britain, and land around the Arctic Ocean, for example, have wide shelves. Where the land bordering the ocean is mountainous, as along the west coasts of North and South America, the continental shelf is narrow. Continental shelves are only about eight per cent of the area of the oceans.

Although the continental shelf is covered by water, it is actually part of the coastal land. The edge of the ocean has moved back and forth over it as the sea-level has risen and fallen. At times during the last ice age when the sea-level was 400 feet lower than it is now, the shoreline must have been at the shelf break with the whole continental shelf above water. Some features now found under water on the shelf – for example, peat now under water along the eastern United States – must have been formed when the shelf was exposed. The seaward break of the continental shelf in most areas was caused by erosion or by the accumulation of sediment.

Oceanographers have studied continental shelves in detail not only because they are close to land but because they are rich in resources. The waters over the continental shelves abound with sea life and most of the world's fishing is done there. The rocks under them are an important source of oil and natural gas. About a quarter of the world's supply comes from there at present and in the future this will increase at a time when supplies on land are running out.

depending on the size of the particles of which it is made. As with much of the ocean bottom, it might have ripple marks or channels in it where it had been moved and shaped by currents in the water.

In width, the continental shelf ranges from almost nothing to a thousand miles, with an average of about forty. It is widest where it borders low-lying land that was once covered by glaciers, or where large rivers empty into the sea. The east coast of

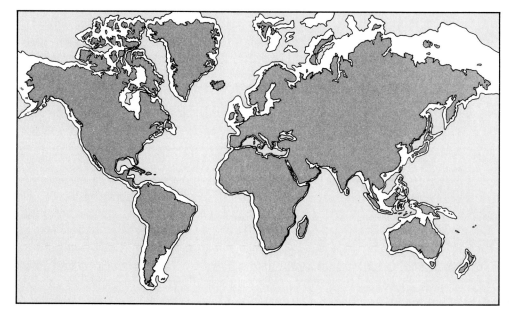

The continental shelves of the whole earth, shown in white

17

Submarine Canyons

Deep valleys, called submarine canyons, cut into the continental slope, the middle section of the continental margin, along many coastlines. These canyons follow a winding path down the slope and may continue as small channels in the rise. Along the west coast of North America where the shelf is narrow, canyons may cut right across the shelf. The Monterey Canyon off central California, for example, begins less than a mile offshore. Most canyons off Europe and the east coast of the United States, where the shelf is wide, begin near its outer edge. Some have tributaries running into the main canyon just as rivers on land do.

In cross-section, canyons are generally V-shaped with a width across the top of several miles and a depth of about a thousand feet. Some are much larger; the Monterey Canyon, for example, is as big as the Grand Canyon of the Colorado River. The

Cable engineers have developed new techniques, such as this cable-laying plow, for protecting undersea cables from turbidity currents and fishermen's nets. The plow buries the cable in the sea floor while being towed along by the mother ship, and the operation is monitored by floodlit TV cameras. The SCUBA-diving cameraman in this picture is taking general shots of the operation.

floor of a typical submarine canyon is flat and covered with sediment, which tends to be especially thick at the far or seaward end.

The similarity between submarine canyons and deep river canyons on land and the location of some undersea canyons at the mouths of large rivers such as the Hudson and the Congo suggest that the rivers may have carved out the canyons when the sea-level was lower than it is today. The upper reaches of many canyons were formed in this way. But as the lower reaches of many canyons are below the lowest level the sea reached during the last ice age, they could not have been cut by land rivers. The thick deposits of sediment at their ends provide a clue to their origin. This sediment must once have been on the continental shelf because it contains the remains of plants and animals that lived there. It was probably swept from the shelf down the slope in dense and swirling currents called turbidity currents. These currents can be triggered by earthquakes or floods which bring large amounts of sediment into the sea. As the sediment slides swiftly down the continental slope, it carries much of the

Placing a profile (blue line – below) of the submarine Monterey Canyon in the Pacific on top of one of the Grand Canyon of the Colorado River (above) gives us an impression of their very similar shapes.

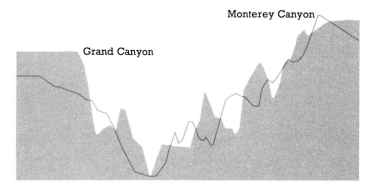

surrounding water with it at speeds of up to fifty miles an hour. Turbidity currents are quite powerful enough to carve out submarine canyons.

In 1929 the force of turbidity currents, caused by an earthquake off the east coast of North America, snapped a series of deep undersea cables.

Ocean Ridges

Deep beneath the sea, vast mountain chains called ridges cover an area almost equal to that of all the land on the earth's surface. Measuring as much as 1000 miles wide, these ocean ridges tower two miles above the deep sea floor, and yet their peaks, or crests, are mostly one to two miles below the surface.

Contrasting sharply with the sloping continental shelves and flat abyssal plains, ridges are the most rugged, bumpy features of the sea floor, with rows of individual ridges on either side of the main crest. Many ocean ridges have a deep steep-sided valley (called a rift or median valley) at their center. These

A detail of the South Atlantic from the BBC television relief model of the world's ocean floor features. The Mid-Atlantic Ridge runs here between South America and Africa.

rift valleys can be up to one mile deep, and are usually between six and ten miles wide. The crests are not continuous over long distances – they are split up by enormous fracture zones where the ocean floor has moved in relation to the ridge, dividing it into segments. At right-angles to the

The islands of the Azores (right) are – like Iceland – a part of the Mid-Atlantic Ridge where the crest rises above sea-level.

The ocean ridge system (below) of the whole world. The thinner lines at right-angles to the ridges are fracture zones, which can be seen clearly in the relief model (left).

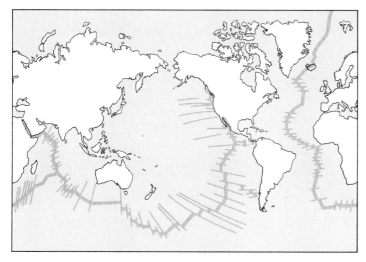

ridge, fracture zones can extend for thousands of miles, as do those running westward from the west coast of North America in the northeastern Pacific.

Before much was known about the depth of the oceans, scientists expected the deepest parts to be at their centers. The discovery of the ocean ridges rising high above the deep sea floor usually near the oceans' centers was therefore quite surprising. The Mid-Atlantic Ridge, which runs the length of the Atlantic near the center, extends north into the Arctic Ocean, and, in two of the rare places where these undersea mountains climb above the level of the water, forms the islands of Iceland and the Azores.

The Mid-Atlantic Ridge stretches south between Africa and Antarctica and into the Indian Ocean, where it becomes the Southwest Indian Ridge, and goes on to a point where it meets two other ridges. North of it, the Carlsberg Ridge (named after the brewery that supported the oceanographic expedition that discovered it) continues between Africa and Arabia into the Gulf of Aden and the Red Sea. The Southeast Indian Ridge follows a course from the Indian Ocean midway between Australia and Antarctica into the Pacific Ocean.

The huge East Pacific Rise, a continuation of the Southeast Indian Ridge, dominates the Pacific Ocean. Unlike most ridges, it is not in the center of the ocean but runs in a curve through the south of the Pacific basin and continues on the eastern side. The East Pacific Rise reaches the North American continent in the Gulf of California, and reappears in the sea farther north off the Oregon coast. The ridges are joined through California by the San Andreas Fault. Movement of the rock on either side of the fault is the cause of earthquakes in this area.

We hardly notice the earthquakes that occur on the ocean ridges as they are far away from land and below sea-level and less destructive than land earthquakes. Volcanoes on the ridges, however, are much more noticeable. A volcano on the Mid-Atlantic Ridge, southwest of Iceland, erupted in 1963 and in a short time built up a completely new island, now named Surtsey.

Seamounts

The ocean plains are not only bordered by high mountain ranges – the ocean ridges – but also dotted with free-standing underwater mountains. These are the seamounts, built up by a series of volcanic eruptions, and sometimes approaching or even breaking the surface. Most of them rise from the flat ocean floor, but some are on an ocean ridge. All have very steep sides and are usually roughly circular. The biggest, such as the island of Hawaii, rise more than five miles – about as high as Mount Everest – from the seabed and form volcanic islands above sea-level.

Seamounts occur in all the oceans but they are especially numerous in the Pacific, where there are more than 10,000. There are so many seamounts that oceanographers have trouble thinking up names for them. One, near the US west coast is called simply the California Seamount. Another is named after the

The inactive craters of seamounts Raiatea and Taka'a in the Society Islands break the surface of the Pacific to form a pair of coral-reef-fringed islands. The peaks will slowly sink until only the reefs remain as atolls.

This detail of the BBC relief model shows the northern Pacific, with the Hawaiian chain (right) meeting the Emperor chain (left) at the bend in the center.

research ship that found it, the Discovery Seamount, and many are named after famous people, such as the Plato, Darwin, and Beethoven Seamounts, or after oceanographers, such as the Smith Seamount in the western Pacific near Japan.

Like land volcanoes, seamounts often occur in chains – some straight and some with a bend. The Emperor-Hawaiian chain in the northern Pacific is one of the best-known and the most striking of the bent chains. The southern part forms the Hawaiian

Islands and there the seamounts are active. Farther northwest, the chain turns north and becomes the Emperor chain. Here the seamounts are dormant and most of them lie under the surface. Other major chains in the Pacific run in one or the other of the same directions.

Most seamounts have a sharp peak at the top, but some, called guyots, are flat topped. We know that waves flattened these guyots by wearing away the peaks that reached above sea-level. But many guyots now lie below the surface and often below the lowest sea-level of the last ice age – some are as much as a mile below the present sea-level. The guyots may have sunk into the earth's crust under their own weight. Some are going down with the whole ocean floor where it is sinking as it gets older and cools.

Types of seamount

Strombolli (Mediterranean): an active volcano above sea-level

San Juan Seamount (105 miles off the Californian coast): a typical submerged seamount

Sylvania Guyot (Ralik chain, Marshall Islands): the peak had been worn flat by waves before the whole seamount sank

Bikini Atoll (Ralik chain, Marshall Islands): another guyot, but with its flat top still at sea-level and ringed with coral reefs

Hawaii: an island formed by several volcanoes rising above the surface of the sea

Abyssal Plains

There are no plains on land that are as large or as flat as the abyssal plains under the ocean. These featureless areas of flat sediment form the main ocean floor, starting at the bottom of the continental rise and running on at a very gentle incline of up to six feet per mile, until they meet a mid-ocean ridge. The depth below sea-level of an abyssal plain is much the same all over it, but there are variations between one plain and another.

The Atlantic contains several abyssal plains, including the Hatteras and Sohm plains off North America, the Madeira, Canary and Cape Verde plains off Africa, the Argentine plain off South America, and the Angola plain off southern Africa. The eastern Pacific is mostly occupied by the submarine mountains of the East Pacific Rise, but the western Pacific has large areas of abyssal plains, although many of them have their flatness broken by numbers of underwater peaks and volcanoes.

The floor of the abyssal plains is covered with sediments and it is these that give the plains their smoothness. Thanks to the technique of seismic profiling, oceanographers have been able to map features that lie below the sediments and we now know that blanketed beneath them there are whole mountains – the older parts of ocean ridges. Some of the peaks of these sediment-covered ridges have remained clear above the level of the plain, and are called abyssal hills.

The main abyssal plains in the Atlantic can be recognized as the lighter-colored areas on the BBC television relief model (right). They lie on both sides of the mid-ocean ridge, between it and the blue-colored continental shelves.

The results of a seismic reflection survey of the Madeira abyssal plain in the northeast Atlantic revealed old sea floor ranges lying beneath the level sediments. This visual record published in 1971 projects a seventy-mile profile, with heights exaggerated by a factor of twenty. The seismic waves sensed to a depth of over 21,500 feet below sea-level. A peak was detected above the ocean floor, topping 16,800 feet below sea-level.

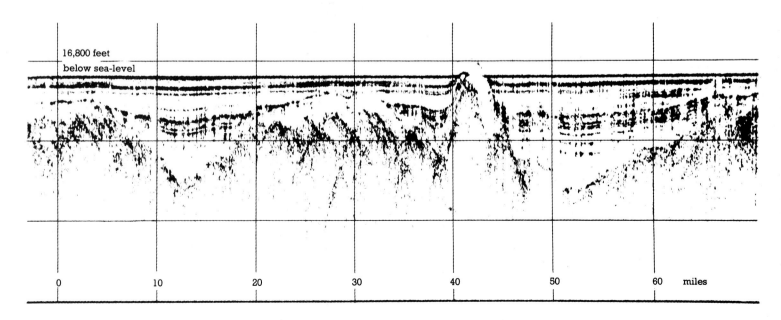

16,800 feet
below sea-level

0   10   20   30   40   50   60   miles

Sea Floor Sediments

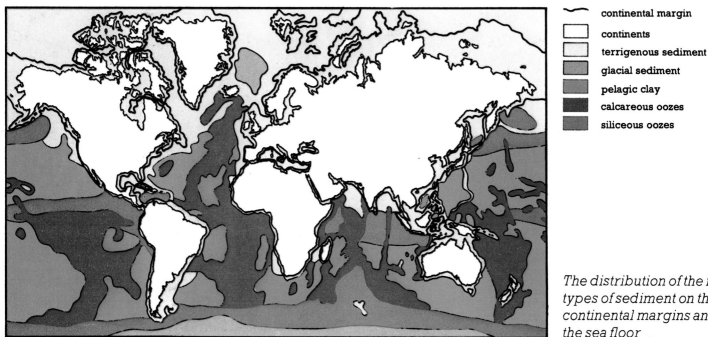

—	continental margin
□	continents
	terrigenous sediment
	glacial sediment
	pelagic clay
	calcareous oozes
	siliceous oozes

The distribution of the five types of sediment on the continental margins and the sea floor

Most of the ocean floor is covered with a sediment made up of fragments of rock and dust from the land and the remains of sea organisms that have dropped through the water to the seabed. Sediment accumulation is usually thickest near land. The only areas that have none have been swept clean by strong currents or are new sea floor which has not yet accumulated any.

Most sediment from the land, called terrigenous sediment, is carried in rivers to the sea where currents pick it up and deposit it fairly close to the land. Because it consists of particles of gravel, sand and mud, it is relatively coarse. Large amounts tend to accumulate around river mouths; in the Indian Ocean, for example, there are thick deposits where the Ganges and Indus Rivers empty. The continent of Antarctica also has a thick belt of terrigenous sediment around it. This sediment reached the ocean in ice that formed on land, broke off into the sea, drifted into warmer water and melted.

Turbidity currents are another source of terrigenous sediment on the abyssal plains. As they flow down a continental slope, turbidity currents carry large amounts of sediment from the continental shelf down into the deeper sea. They slow down at the base of the continental slope where most of their sediment remains, forming the continental rise, but some of the sediment is carried farther out to sea through channels in the rise. This sediment is then slowly deposited in level beds called turbidites, which make much of the plains so flat. A turbidite bed will have coarser sediments at the bottom, where the heavier parts of the sediment dropped first, and a covering of finer silt or clay at the top. A turbidite bed may be between a few inches and a foot in thickness, and the average rate of build-up is not more than an inch or two each thousand years. Turbidity currents do not occur often.

Pelagic (open-ocean) sediment covers much more of the ocean floor than does terrigenous sediment – about three-quarters of it. Pelagic sediment contains tiny grains of material that sink very slowly through the water. There are two main types: clay and ooze. Clay consists of particles less than one-thousandth of an inch in diameter that are picked up by winds over land, especially deserts, and swept over the ocean. These particles eventually drop out of the atmosphere or are washed out by rain, fall into the ocean, and sink to the bottom. Other ingredients of pelagic clay include dust from volcanic eruptions that falls into the ocean thousands of miles away, and meteorites that have fallen from space. Pelagic clay accumulates at a rate of about one-thousandth of an inch every thousand years. Over millions of years, however, a layer hundreds of feet thick has accumulated in some parts of the ocean floor.

The pelagic oozes have a different kind of origin; they are the remains of minute plants and animals (called plankton) that live, or have lived, in the sea. The hard parts that remain when these creatures die sink to the sea floor, together with the particles of pelagic clay. However, the shells and skeletons that form the ooze accumulate much faster than the clay, and add about an inch every thousand years. The remains of plankton which are composed of calcium carbonate (calcareous oozes) are the most abundant of all pelagic sediments. A smaller amount comes from remains which are composed of silica (siliceous oozes). Both kinds of ooze are white or light in color, unlike the clays, which are brown due to the presence of iron in the sediment. The quantities and kinds of plankton and the depth of the water decide the type of pelagic ooze found on the sea floor.

Because ocean floor sediment has been accumulating for millions of years, it holds clues to conditions in the oceans in the past. The organisms whose remains help form the sediment, for example, have evolved over time. By examining these remains, we can tell how old the sediment is. And because some live only in cold water and some only in warm, we can trace the pattern of temperature changes in the ocean and find the periods of ice ages.

Radiolarians like these (magnified almost four hundred times), together with other creatures composed of silica, make up the siliceous oozes.

The tiny plates (left) magnified by scanning electron microscope measure one 2000th of a millimeter across. They are the remains of the shells of phytoplankton called coccolithophores. Together with remains of the zooplankton called foraminifera (above magnified 4.25 times), they are the main constituents of calcareous oozes.

The Deepest Part

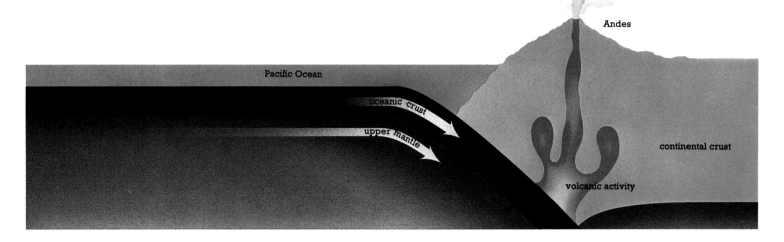

Pacific Ocean

oceanic crust

upper mantle

Andes

continental crust

volcanic activity

A simplified section of the Peru–Chile Trench. Here we see the reason for earthquakes and volcanoes in an area of ocean trenches: a slab consisting of oceanic crust and the upper part of the earth's mantle is plunging into the interior of the earth, and partly turning into molten rock underneath the continent. The movement of the slabs causes earthquakes and some of the molten rock is forced up to the surface to form volcanoes. The Andes mountain range (left) was raised by these movements close to the Peru-Chile trench, and contains many active volcanoes.

The deepest parts of the oceans are the trenches, which rim some parts of the edges of all oceans, but almost completely encircle the Pacific. The Tonga and Kermadec Trenches just north of New Zealand cross its southern side. The Mariana, Philippine and Japan Trenches run along the west, and the Aleutian Trench between Siberia and Alaska borders the north. On the eastern side there are trenches off the west coasts of Central and South America. The Atlantic has smaller trenches in the Caribbean Sea and near the southern tip of South America, and the Java

Trench lies along the northeastern edge of the Indian Ocean. Trenches run either parallel to the edge of a continent, or on the open-ocean side of island arcs, where they bulge outward.

When a trench borders the mainland, it lies along the bottom of the continental slope where the continental rise usually is found. Continental margins with trenches are very different from those without – they have almost no continental shelves, steeper continental slopes, and no continental rise. On the nearby land there is usually a high range of mountains with

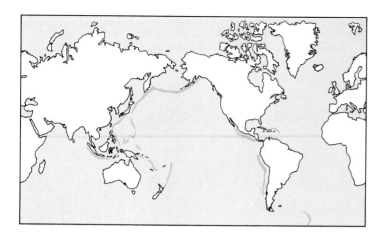

The position of ocean trenches throughout the world : island-arc trenches are shown in blue and mainland-edge trenches in black.

The Aleutian Islands in the North Pacific, with the Aleutian Trench on their outward-curving side, present the typical structure of an island arc. Along this line, the main Pacific plate is thrusting in a north-westerly direction underneath the Bering Sea.

volcanoes running parallel to the trench. The Peru–Chile Trench, for example, borders the mountains of the Andes which run the length of the western coast of South America. It descends to a slightly greater depth (nearly 26,500 feet) below sea-level than the height to which the Andes rise above sea-level. The Challenger Deep, in the Mariana Trench in the western Pacific, is where the submersible *Trieste* reached a depth of more than 35,800 feet in 1960.

Trenches are about fifty miles wide and may be thousands of miles long. The Peru–Chile Trench, the longest, stretches for 5000 miles. In cross-section, they are lopsided Vs with the steep side of the V on the land or island side and a gentler slope on the open-ocean side. There is usually a narrow, flat plain covered with sediment at the bottom.

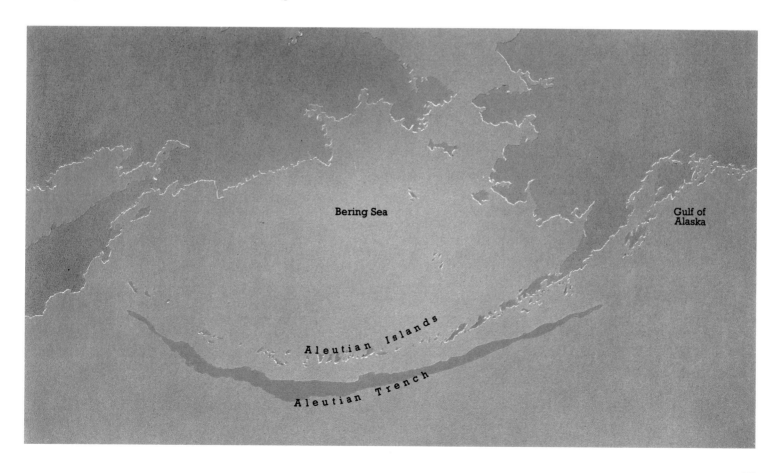

Bering Sea

Gulf of Alaska

Aleutian Islands

Aleutian Trench

Evolution of the Oceans

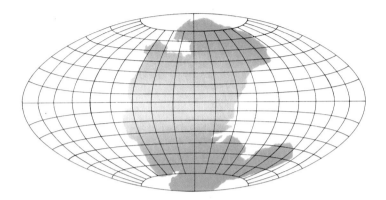

About 220 million years ago the present-day continents formed a single supercontinent (called Pangaea by earth-scientists).

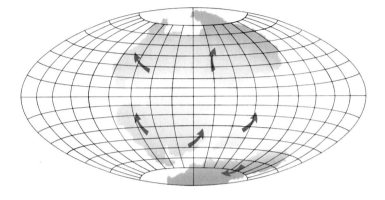

About 100 million years ago oceans began to appear in the cracks as the supercontinent gradually broke up and moved away.

A theory linking some of the main features of the present-day oceans – particularly the ridges and trenches – with other evidence from geology seems to explain the origin and shape of the oceans. Called plate tectonics, this theory was developed in the 1960s and is widely regarded as the most comprehensive model we now have for understanding how the earth's crust behaves. Plate tectonics says that all the ocean floors are spreading, pushed apart along the ocean ridges, and that new ocean floor is continually being created by lava welling up in the crack at the center and cooling as new rock.

The existing ocean floor is in movement as part of a larger system of movements by six large plates and many smaller plates which make up the whole of the earth's surface – both oceans and landmasses. As they move, the plates not only pull away from each other at the ocean ridges, but also push toward each other at the other side. Wherever this happens, one plate may either dip under another (as in the Peru-Chile trench) or try to slide past it (as in the San Andreas Fault). Their motion causes earthquakes and volcanic eruptions.

It has been noted that a symmetry exists on either side of the central part of the ridge. This is a result of new material being added along the center and pushing aside the old material more or less equally on both sides. The top of the ridge is free from sediment, for the rocks there are too young to have accumulated a layer of it. We also find the reason why even the oldest parts of the present sea floors (200 million years) are young in comparison with the age of the rest of the earth: as new floor was created, the older crust at the edge of the ocean basin was pushed away and destroyed – forced under the deep ocean trenches where it was melted down. This is known to be happening along the Andes (the Peru-Chile Trench) and also to have created the island arc of Japan where two plates collide.

One of the most striking things that anyone can see on a map of the Atlantic Ocean is the way that South America and Africa appear to be two interconnecting pieces of a jigsaw puzzle that have moved apart and are now separated by water. This apparent fitting of the continents together led to a proposal early this century that the continents had once been attached but had drifted apart, and that continents were lighter than the oceans and floated on them. Plate tectonics differs from this so-called 'continental drift' theory in that the moving parts are not just continents but plates that carry both continents and oceans. Scientific research confirms that the ocean basins are not fixed in their position or size, but are in the process of opening and closing.

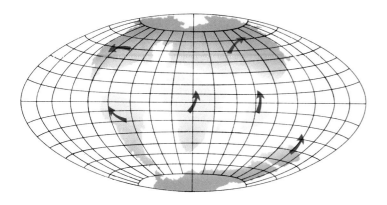

About 50 million years ago the Atlantic was growing in size, and India was migrating toward Asia.

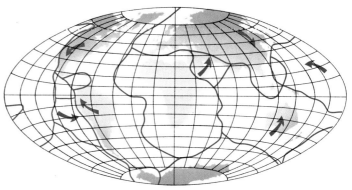

Today the margins of the plates as shown here are still active, some of them carrying the continents on their backs to new destinations.

A new ocean in the making: the Red Sea (bottom) and the Gulf of Aden, seen in a satellite photograph looking south, are widening as Africa (right) and Arabia drift apart.

Formation of the Pacific

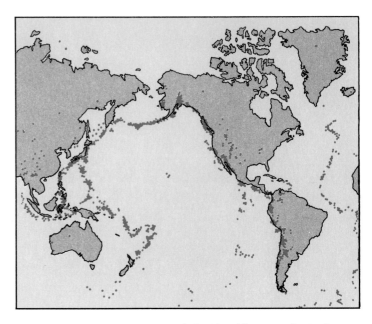

Earthquakes in and around the Pacific are plotted on this map to show where the edges of the earth's moving plates crunch together. Each dot shows an earthquake recorded by the US Coast and Geodetic Survey in the years 1961–7.

The Pacific Ocean now covers about a third of the earth's surface. In the past it was even larger, and it has been decreasing in area as a result of its floor being pushed under neighboring plates and destroyed. When all the land masses formed a single supercontinent, the Pacific could then be said to have covered all the rest of the globe as a single super-ocean. About 200 million years ago, when the super-continent began to split up, North America moved north and west. About fifty million years later South America followed. Eurasia also moved toward the east. The Atlantic Ocean began to grow ever wider between them. About 100 million years ago Australia was joined to Antarctica. Around seventy million years ago the Tasman Sea opened, separating New Zealand from Australia, and about fifty-five million years ago sea floor spreading started between Antarctica and Australia, and Australia began to move north.

It is difficult to predict what will happen to the Pacific Ocean in the future. It is much easier to tell what has happened in the past.

There are ocean trenches on three sides of the Pacific Ocean – to the west, north, and east – and there the Pacific plate is sinking into the earth at the rate of up to four inches a year. Nearly a square mile of floor is being destroyed each year. This may not seem very fast, but geological time is very long. The oldest parts of the Pacific floor in the west, near the Caroline Islands, are almost 200 million years old; therefore the Pacific must have substantially decreased in size since then.

Besides losing floor at its edges, the Pacific has the East Pacific Rise – the world's fastest-spreading ridge. Plates on either side of it are separating at up to six inches a year, making new ocean floor. (The Mid-Atlantic Ridge spreads at about an inch a year.) But in spite of the East Pacific Rise spreading so fast, the Pacific is still contracting through the destruction at the trenches on either side of the ocean.

In the western Pacific seamounts are a major feature, many of them forming chains. These chains are caused by repeated volcanic eruptions at a fixed point as the plate moves over a source of molten rock below it, called a hot spot – like a sewing-machine needle stabbing a piece of cloth as it moves past. These chains are all roughly parallel to each other and show the direction that the Pacific plate is moving, toward the northwest, the bend in many of the seamount chains being caused by a small change in direction of the movement of the plate.

The life story of the Pacific Ocean plate and the mechanics of how it moves are broadly visualized in this diagram. Under the earth's surface (shown as if cut open) the advance of new sea floor can be followed from where it is formed at the ridge until it is swallowed up millions of years later under the trenches. The ages of different parts of the floor are given in millions of years. The oldest are farthest away from the ridge.

Seawater

The earth has more than 300 million cubic miles of water. Most of it is in the oceans, but some is on loan to the atmosphere, to the glaciers and ice caps, and to the land. Water is being transferred continuously between the oceans, the atmosphere and the land in what is called the hydrologic cycle. Water evaporating from both the oceans and land condenses into water droplets in clouds, and falls back as rain or snow. This is called "precipitation." The sea loses more water through evaporation than returns as rain over the sea, while the opposite is usually true for land areas. The cycle is therefore adding more water to the land than is returned to the ocean, but this is balanced by water in rivers flowing off the land to replenish the ocean.

So if most rainwater comes from the sea, why isn't it salty? Seawater has solid substances dissolved in it, but when seawater evaporates, only the pure water is taken up into the atmosphere. The solid

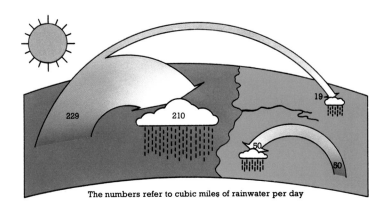

The numbers refer to cubic miles of rainwater per day

This simplified diagram shows the evaporation and rainfall "budget" in which land gains water from the ocean. Balance is restored chiefly by water flowing off the land in rivers and underground seepage to the sea. Rain from the land may fall over the sea, but the amount, world-wide, is infinitesimal.

An Ice Patrol vessel tows an iceberg out of a shipping lane off Greenland where it could be a hazard. Icebergs may one day be towed like this for thousands of miles to arid regions where they could be melted down as pure water.

substances remain behind in the sea.

Because of the dissolved substances in it, seawater must be colder than pure water to freeze: while pure water freezes at 32°F, the temperature of seawater must drop to about 28°F to freeze. (This principle is used when antifreeze is added to the water in a car radiator – the antifreeze lowers the freezing-point of the water.) When ice begins to form on seawater, the solid substances drop out of the ice to the unfrozen water below. Sea ice, therefore, is made of pure water.

The formation of ice on the ocean surface is a gradual process in several stages. Small crystals of ice form first and then join together into thin platelets called pancake ice. Finally, the pancakes freeze together to form an ice shelf or floe ranging from six to ten feet thick. Ice sheets that survive the summer become even thicker and stronger when the water of melted ice that lay on its surface freezes again.

Sea ice looks blue in color and is bumpy where it has broken or been deformed by the wind. Ice is lighter than unfrozen water. It floats on the surface and protects the water below from the cold air above,

slowing down the freezing process. Submarines have sailed under polar ice in the warmer waters below.

Icebergs, one of the most magnificent sights in the ocean, are not made of sea ice, but are huge chunks of glaciers on the Antarctic continent or the land around the Arctic Ocean which have broken off at the point where these glaciers meet the ocean. Winds and currents carry them out to sea. About 12,000 icebergs break off the Greenland ice cap in the Arctic each year and drift out into the North Atlantic, where they become a hazard to shipping because they are so large. They are tracked by the International Ice Patrol, which was founded by international agreement in 1913, a year after the luxury liner *Titanic* hit a small iceberg and sank.

These maps show how the sub-zero polar regions lock up increasing amounts of seawater in the form of sea ice as the northern and southern winters advance. The ice caps remain on Greenland and the Antarctic continent all the year round.

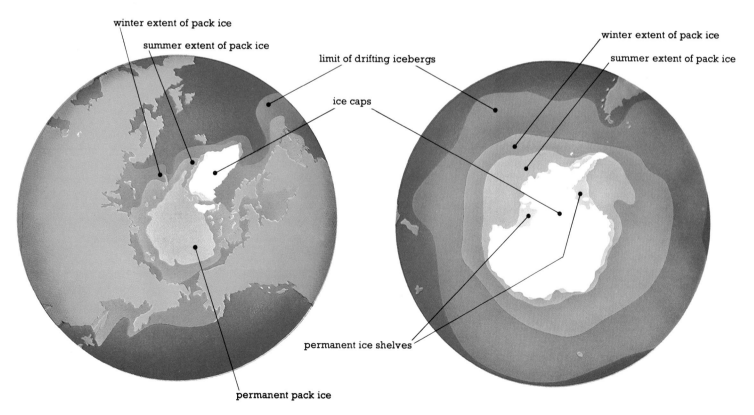

winter extent of pack ice
summer extent of pack ice
limit of drifting icebergs
ice caps
winter extent of pack ice
summer extent of pack ice
permanent ice shelves
permanent pack ice

Sea Salt

Seawater differs from pure water in that it has solid substances dissolved in it. Although almost all the elements are present, the two most abundant are sodium and chlorine, the ingredients of common salt. These and four other elements – magnesium, sulphur, calcium and potassium – make up more than ninety per cent in weight of the chemical elements dissolved in seawater. The other elements are present only in extremely small quantities.

The salinity of seawater depends on the amount of these chemical elements dissolved in it and is measured in the number of parts of the elements in one thousand parts of water. In the open ocean, salinity ranges from thirty-three to thirty-seven parts per thousand, with an average of thirty-five, or three and a half per cent. Higher percentages occur where evaporation removes much of the pure water, leaving behind the elements, and where water is enclosed and cannot mix with the open ocean. The Red Sea, for example, is partly enclosed and has higher than average salinity. Lower than average salinity occurs in coastal areas where large rivers empty into the sea, and in polar regions during the season when melting ice dilutes the seawater.

Differences of climate also affect the cycle of evaporation and precipitation. Near the Equator high temperatures increase evaporation, but rainfall is plentiful and salinity stays relatively low. Between these regions and about 40° north and south, salinity is high because rainfall is not great enough to replace the water removed by evaporation. In the polar regions salinity begins to drop as snow and rain increase and cold weather reduces evaporation. Climate does not affect the lower depths of the ocean below 3000 feet and salinity there remains constant at about thirty-five parts per thousand in all the oceans.

Although salinity varies from one area of open ocean to another, the ratio of the six most abundant elements, shown in the adjoining table, and bromine, strontium and boron remains the same to each other. This means that scientists can determine the quantity of only one of these elements and use this to calculate the amounts of the others and therefore the salinity of the water. Chlorine, the most abundant and easily measured element, was in general use for this purpose until salinity began to be measured by the faster and more accurate process of electrical conductivity.

The quantities of the less abundant elements in seawater vary because marine plants use some of them and can deplete the supply. The most important of these elements are carbon and dissolved oxygen, which combine to form the gas carbon dioxide.

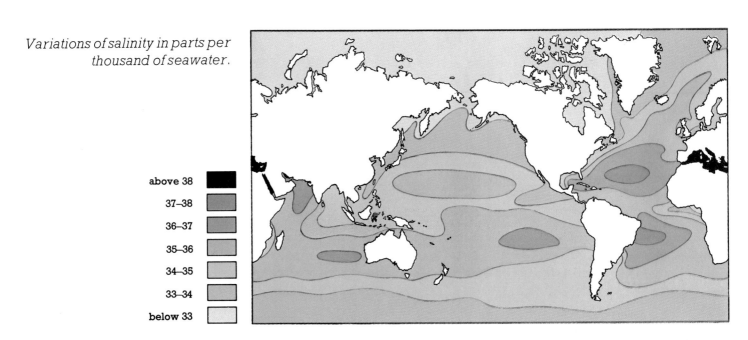

Variations of salinity in parts per thousand of seawater.

above 38
37–38
36–37
35–36
34–35
33–34
below 33

Microscopic floating plants containing the green substance chlorophyll use the sun's energy with carbon dioxide and water to produce sugar on which the plants feed. This process is called photosynthesis. Plants also need other chemical substances, called nutrients, for growth, and although these are available in tiny, almost undetectable amounts – about one part per billion parts – they are essential to sustain life in the sea.

A natural salt pan among the rocks of Dwejra Bay, on Gozo Island near Malta. The sun's extreme heat evaporates any seawater that washes in from the cove, leaving glistening salt crystals on the sand.

element	parts per thousand
chlorine	19.5
sodium	10.77
magnesium	1.29
sulphur	0.905
calcium	0.412
potassium	0.380
bromine	0.067
carbon	0.028
nitrogen	0.0115
strontium	0.008
oxygen	0.006
boron	0.0044
silicon	0.002
fluorine	0.0013

A table of the concentration of the chemical elements in seawater. The other elements are present in less than 0.001 parts per thousand.

Waves

An Atlantic wave breaking as it comes in to the shore on Long Island, N.Y. In the open sea, the crests of waves will only break on an obstruction or if there is a strong wind blowing.

The waves that roll ashore on most beaches and cause ships at sea to rise and fall are one of the most familiar characteristics of the sea. Ranging in size from ripples to towering masses of water over fifty feet high, they help shape our shoreline by forming and reforming beaches, cliffs, and sand dunes. In storms, they can even destroy everything in their path. New machines can harness their energy and use it to generate electricity.

Waves are described by measuring their wave length – the distance between two crests – and their wave height – the distance between the bottom of the wave trough and the top of the crest. The highest open sea wave ever measured – it was in the Pacific – had a wave height of 112 feet.

The main cause of waves is wind blowing across the surface of the ocean. The speed of the wind, the length of the time it has been blowing, and the distance it has traveled across the open ocean determine the height of the wave. Deep-water sailors have long had a rule of thumb that uses the wave height to estimate the wind speed; the wave height in feet is about half the wind speed in knots. In 1806 the British admiral Sir Francis Beaufort improved on this rule by estimating wind speed from the condition of the sea and the sky. The result was the wind scale named for him, with a Beaufort Number for each of twelve wind strengths. Related originally to the amount of sail a fully rigged warship could carry in a wind of each strength, the scale is still in use today in shipping forecasts.

Waves indicate that there is movement in the water, but this does not mean, however, that water moves along with the waves. A swimmer floating on water beyond the point where the waves are breaking rises and falls with the waves as they pass, but he does not move along with them toward the shore. Only a current, which is a whole mass of seawater on the move, could cause that. Boats also bob up and down with the waves but do not move along. The basic motion of the water is roughly circular, rising like a wheel to meet each crest as it comes along and falling when it passes. Waves are the result of water changing shape, not of water flowing with the wind.

Beaufort Number	description of wind	condition of sea	wind speed (mph)	wave height (feet)
0	Calm	Sea like a mirror	less than 1	0
1	Light air	Ripples; no foam crests	1-3	0.5
2	Light breeze	Wavelets; crests do not break	4-7	1
3	Gentle breeze	Foam glassy, not yet white	8-12	2
4	Moderate breeze	Waves longer; white crests	13-18	5
5	Fresh breeze	Waves pronounced and long; many foam crests	19-24	10
6	Strong breeze	Larger waves; white foam crests	25-31	15
7	Moderate gale	Sea heaps up; wind blows foam in streaks	32-38	20
8	Fresh gale	High waves and crests	39-46	25
9	Strong gale	Foam blown in dense streaks	47-54	30
10	Whole gale	High waves; long crests; large foam patches	55-63	35
11	Storm	High waves; deep troughs	64-75	—
12	Hurricane	Sea covered with streaky foam; air filled with spray	above 75	—

The Beaufort Wind Scale 1–12 with sea conditions in summarized form, and approximate speeds and heights of waves.

And the water involved in this movement is only surface water – at depths greater than half the wave length, the water moves very little.

As waves move into shallow water where the depth is less than half the wave length, the movement of the water changes. The water circulating underneath the crest touches the sea bed, the wave slows down, the wave length shortens, and the wave height increases. When the wave height exceeds about a seventh of the wave length (or, put another way, when the water depth is 1.3 times the wave height or less), the wave breaks and the water in it rushes toward the shore. The movement of water in a breaking wave, or breaker, is clearly visible along the beach and it sweeps along anyone standing or swimming in it.

An endless chain of identical small waves can be reproduced in a wave tank by a wave machine at one end of it. Oceanographers use them to study how obstacles or changes in depth of water affect the movement of water in waves. The effect of waves on new designs for ships can also be tested. The Pacific Ocean forms a vast natural "wave tank" and has been used to study changes in waves as they travel away from a storm. Oceanographers tracked waves produced by a storm in the Antarctic across the Pacific and finally, two weeks later, to the shores of Alaska after a journey of 11,000 miles. The waves had traveled half way around the earth.

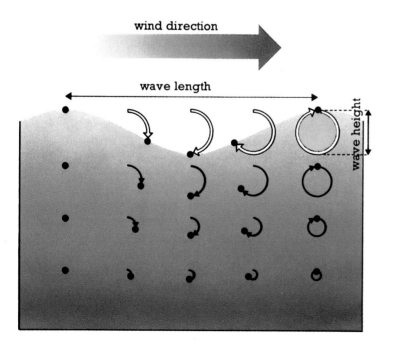

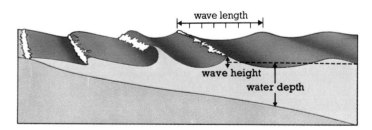

One-half of the wave length is the critical depth (shown between arrows) in shallow water at which a wave begins its sequence of cresting and breaking.

The imaginary circles in this diagram represent the general movement of corresponding water particles within a wave system. The farther down from the surface the particles are, the smaller and slower do their circular paths become.

Catastrophic Waves

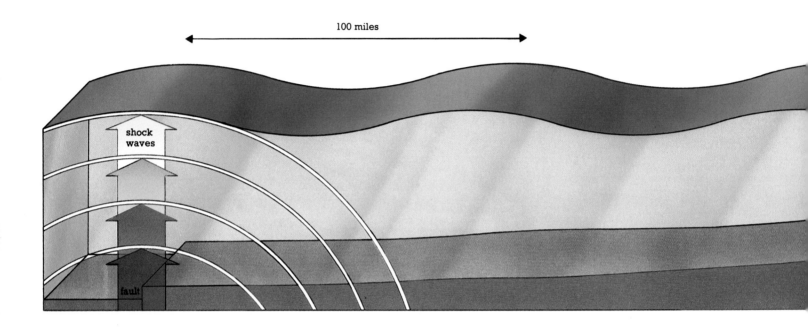

100 miles

shock waves

fault

The most spectacular and destructive waves in the ocean, commonly called tidal waves, have nothing to do with tides, as the name implies, or with wind as do most other waves. They are due to earthquakes and undersea volcanoes. Oceanographers prefer to call them by their Japanese name, tsunami. During an earthquake the seabed can move suddenly, displacing a large mass of water, disturbing the sea's surface, and setting up a train of tsunamis that travels away from the center of the earthquake. Undersea volcanoes can set up the same series of movements.

The crests of tsunamis are often a hundred miles or more apart. Because they travel at speeds of up to 450 miles per hour, however, one will pass a given point about every fifteen minutes. In the open sea they are no more than a few feet high and cause little damage; ships can ride over them unaware. When the waves reach shallow water, however, they change. Here the racing waters of the tsunamis are slowed down abruptly. Instead of racing forward, they push up, swelling to thirty feet or more in height

until they break and crash against the shore. Many are harmless, but in some places the shape of the sea floor concentrates their energy in such a way that they grow to terrifying heights of up to a hundred feet, causing devastation where their water thunders onto the shore. Sometimes the first wave in a train is the biggest; sometimes it is a later one.

Tsunamis have brought tremendous destruction to many parts of the world. Because the Pacific has so many volcanic eruptions and earthquakes, however, that is where they are most likely to occur. One of the most famous trains of tsunamis began with a volcanic explosion on the island of Krakatoa in what is now Indonesia in 1883. Tsunamis more than a hundred feet high crashed onto nearby islands and in one case swept a gunboat two miles inland. In 1946 another train of tsunamis, caused by an earthquake near the Aleutian Islands in the North Pacific, destroyed a lighthouse forty-five feet above sea-level and a radio tower more than a hundred feet above sea-level on Unimak Island. The same tsunamis

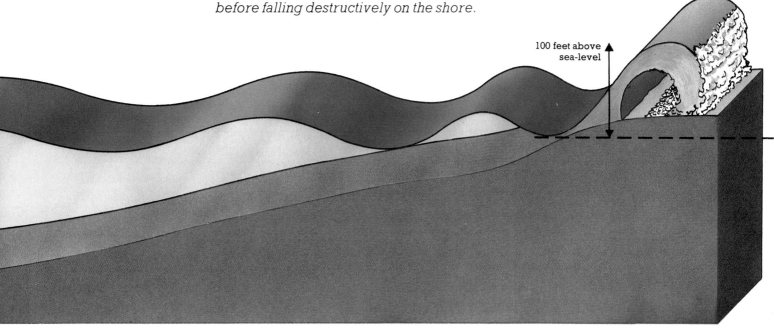

The terrible force of a tsunami is generated by the exceptional length and speed of the waves, making it quite different from even the worst storm-waves produced by the wind. This schematic diagram shows how, as the waves reach the shallows, the water is piled up into a series of mountainous walls of water, before falling destructively on the shore.

100 feet above sea-level

went on to cause severe damage in Hawaii five hours later. Tsunamis in the Atlantic, caused by an earthquake in Lisbon in Portugal in 1755, smashed ships in the harbor and lifted huge amounts of water onto the land. The water destroyed much of what was left of the city after the earthquake and swept many of the survivors out to sea.

The only protection against the devastating effects of some tsunamis is an early warning that they are coming. Since 1946 a warning system has helped protect land areas in the Pacific. Through a world-wide network of detectors, it can pinpoint the location of an earthquake within a few minutes and predict the time any tsunamis that result would arrive at various coasts. Because most earthquakes do not cause tsunamis there are many false alarms. However, when tsunamis are detected in one area the warning service can predict accurately when they will arrive at others.

The tsunami that ravaged Hilo on Hawaii Island on 23 May 1960 scooped this boulder from the sea and dropped it ashore.

Tides

The gravitational pull of the moon and the sun on earth and the rotation of the earth cause the level of the water in the oceans to change. This pull affects the atmosphere and the land also, but it is only visible in the oceans where it causes the sometimes dramatic rise of water level called the tide. The pull is greatest on the side of the earth facing the moon. On the side away from the moon, where its pull is weakest, the water bulges away from the moon, causing a corresponding high tide.

While the moon rotates around the earth once in

Mont Saint-Michel off the Brittany coast at low tide. When the tide is high, it becomes an island.

every twenty-eight days, it takes twenty-four hours and fifty minutes for the earth to rotate in relation to the moon. During this latter period, a place on earth faces the moon once and faces away from the moon once and therefore most places have two high tides. Because the earth's own rotation takes twenty-four hours, high tides slip fifty minutes later each day.

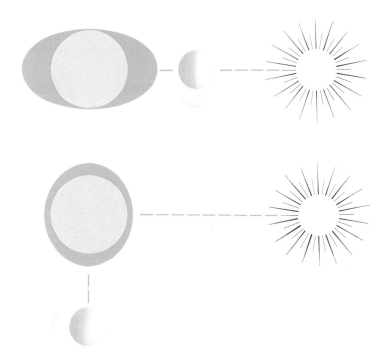

This simplified diagram shows how the relative positions of the sun and the moon create the tides in the earth's oceans. It also shows that water on the side opposite to the main gravitational pull from the moon surges in a high tide.

The bore in the Ch'ien-t'ang Chiang estuary near Hangchow in China has a height of up to eleven feet, and travels upriver at about ten knots.

Although most parts of the earth have two high and two low tides every twenty-four hours, a few have only one high and one low and some have a mixture of the two, with one high tide being much higher than the other. These differences are due to latitude, the effect of different depths of the ocean, the shape of a coastline, and the angles of the moon and sun relative to the Equator.

The sun is much farther away and its effect on the tide is less than half that of the moon. When both the sun and the moon face the same side of the earth at the same time, their pull is then increased and very high tides, called spring tides, result. When the sun and moon form a right-angle with the earth, the gravitational pulls of the two are in opposition, causing weaker tides, called neap tides. Spring tides and neap tides occur every fourteen days – spring tides when the moon is new and full and neap tides during the moon's first and third quarters. Since tides depend on the movement of the earth and the moon, the times of high and low water can usually be predicted accurately to within a few minutes.

The difference between the high water level and the low water level of a tide is known as the tidal range which varies from time to time and from place to place. The widest tidal range in the world is at the head of the Bay of Fundy on the east coast of Canada, where it reaches sixty feet. The Mediterranean, by contrast, has a very narrow tidal range. In the English Channel, the range in most places is about five feet, while in the Bristol Channel south of Wales it can reach forty feet. The Gulf of Mexico has a tidal range of only a few feet, while in the Pacific, less than a hundred miles away at the closest point, the range is about fifteen feet.

Where there are wide tidal ranges, large amounts of water flow in what are called tidal currents. In the open ocean, tidal currents travel at less than a quarter of a knot, but in coastal waters, if these are shallow or narrow, the speed may reach several knots. In the days of sailing ships, sailors used these currents to help them leave port by sailing "with the tide." Many vessels still follow this practice today, and it helps supertankers to maneuver in shallow moorings.

Where strong tidal currents flow into shallow water at the mouth of a river, the incoming water can form a fast-moving mass of water with an almost vertical wave front called a "bore" which rushes upriver.

Winds and Currents

The local currents we know on coasts and in shallow water are largely the result of the rise and fall of the tide, but farther out to sea there is a worldwide system of large, continuous currents that roughly fit the pattern of the earth's prevailing winds.

Winds result from differences in air temperature and from the fact that hotter air becomes lighter and rises while colder air becomes heavier and sinks. Hot air at the Equator rises and is replaced by cooler air from higher latitudes flowing in as winds. Cold air at the Poles sinks and moves toward the Equator. If the earth were not rotating, all the air on the earth's surface would flow from the Poles toward the Equator. However, the earth's rotation pulls the

As fuel costs soar, seamen and international traders are recalling that wind power is still free. The worldwide pattern of winds may come into use again as it was when this 200-ton barquentine carried freight in the English Channel as late as the 1920s.

winds to the right or the left, forming a more complex pattern.

The two main wind systems of the northern and southern hemispheres are mirror-images of each other: between each side of the Equator and 30° latitude north and south there are the Trade Winds, which blow from the northeast in the northern

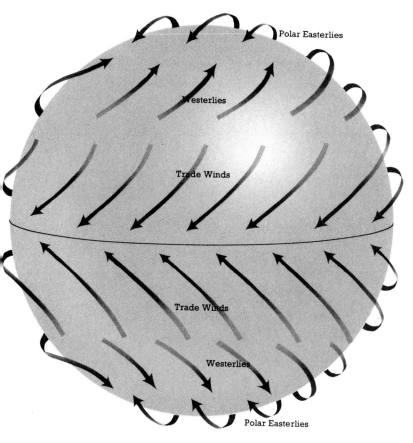

The Trade Winds and the Westerlies do two things to the seas over which they blow: they push the surface up and down by raising waves, and they drag the water itself along in the direction they themselves are going. Since the wind can only skim the surface, the currents created in this way pick up only a small proportion of the wind's energy and move much more slowly. They do not flow directly downwind either, but are deflected to the right or the left by the rotation of the earth, depending on whether the currents are in the northern or southern hemisphere. This deflection of the currents is known as the Coriolis Effect, named after the French mathematician who first analyzed the phenomenon.

The other wind systems are at the Equator and the Poles. Near the Equator is an area of light, variable winds called the Doldrums, in which sailing ships are easily becalmed. The winds that blow at the Poles are the Polar Easterlies. These also create currents, but not such major currents as those caused by the Trade Winds and the Westerlies.

The prevailing winds and the earth's rotation, combined with the landmasses acting as great breakwaters on the currents, produce a pattern of rings of currents circulating in the open oceans; these rings are called gyres.

In the Indian Ocean there is a gyre that breaks the general rule and changes direction with the seasons. Like all gyres, it is controlled by the wind. In the summer the land heats up faster than the Indian Ocean. As the air over the land rises, it is replaced by air moving in from over the sea. This wind, blowing from the southwest and known as the southwest monsoon, creates a clockwise gyre. In winter the opposite is true – the wind changes direction to become the northeast monsoon, which gradually reverses the direction of the gyre until it runs counterclockwise.

A simplified diagram of the earth's wind systems, illustrating the Coriolis Effect, which drags the winds sideways due to the earth's rotation.

hemisphere and from the southeast in the southern. Farther away from the Equator, in the mid-latitudes between 30° and 60° north and south, is the belt of winds called the Westerlies. Trade Winds are so called because in the days of sail trading ships from Europe and Africa to the United States or from the United States to the Orient relied on their consistent direction. On the return journey ships would try to use the power of the Westerlies.

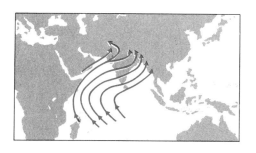

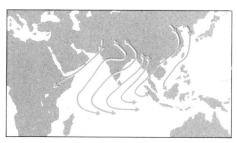

Far left, the southwest monsoon: May–September. Left, the northeast monsoon: October–April.

Surface Currents

The water at the center of each gyre is almost stationary. In the slowly moving waters of an area in the western North Atlantic, known as the Sargasso Sea, vast amounts of seaweed grow. Eels migrate from European waters to live among this seaweed, and return to Europe only to breed.

The currents in each gyre that carry water from the Equator toward the Poles, such as the Gulf Stream and the Kuroshio in the northern hemisphere, are warm. They gradually lose their heat in higher latitudes. The currents that return the water to the Equator, such as the Humboldt and the Benguela in the southern hemisphere, are cooler. Because of this the surface currents moderate our climate, warming cool regions and cooling warm ones.

Currents are fairly weak over most of the ocean surface. Currents on the eastern side of the oceans may reach a speed of one knot, while those on the western side, such as the Gulf Stream, are stronger and may reach as much as five knots. While most wind-driven currents are no more than 300 feet deep, the major currents transport enormous volumes of water. At any given moment the Gulf Stream alone is transporting more than 100 times as much water as all the rivers on earth combined.

As with the wind systems, the gyres in the northern and southern hemispheres resemble each other. They rotate either clockwise or counterclockwise, and usually have a more intense flow on the western side. However, there is a difference, because the ocean currents, unlike the winds, are blocked by the continental landmasses everywhere but in the extreme south.

The gyres are very obvious in the Atlantic Ocean. In the North Atlantic four major currents – the Gulf Stream, the North Atlantic Drift, the Canary Current and the North Equatorial Current – sweep around in a gyre.

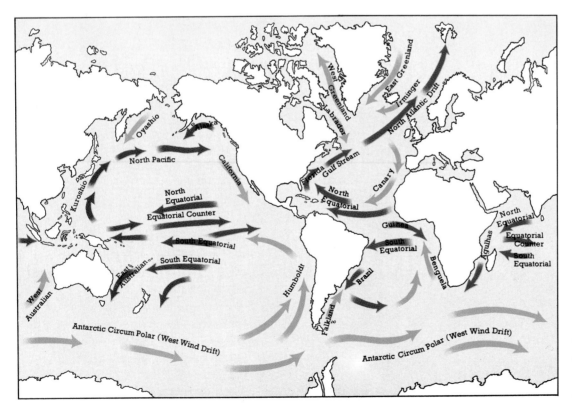

The wind-driven surface currents of the world: red arrows indicate warm currents, blue arrows indicate cold ones.

In the North Pacific is a similar, though more complex, gyre, with the Kuroshio Current, like the Gulf Stream, as the strong western current, running into the North Pacific Current. This gyre meets the southern hemisphere gyre a few degrees north of the Equator in the area of the Doldrums. As there is no strong wind here, a narrow current – the Equatorial Counter Current – is squeezed between the west-flowing North and South Equatorial Currents, and flows eastward. Beyond the major gyres in the southern hemisphere there are no further land

The northwest part of the Gulf Stream, off the coast between Cape Hatteras and Cape Cod, photographed from a satellite, with colors added during development (false-color). Temperatures within the Gulf Stream are coded downward from purple, red and yellow, contrasting with the blues of the cold North Atlantic.

barriers and here the Westerlies whip up the Antarctic Circumpolar Current (also called the West Wind Drift), which runs all the way around the globe.

Currents of the Deep

Although the wind-driven surface currents in the ocean reach down only a few hundred feet, in the two to three miles of water below, deep-water currents also flow. These are driven by the density or weight of the water itself and generally move very slowly, often flowing in a different direction from those on the surface.

The density of water depends on its temperature and its salinity. Colder water and water with greater salinity are heavier and therefore denser than warmer or purer water. Because deep water is cold – its temperature is close to freezing-point even in the tropics where surface water is warm – it is much denser than surface water and has a different pattern of currents. In the Bosporus Straits, for example, the surface water flows westward from the Black Sea toward the Mediterranean, while the water underneath, which is colder and saltier, flows in the opposite direction, that is from west to east.

Surface and deep currents also flow in opposite directions along the Equator; the surface currents flow westward while undercurrents 300 feet down flow eastward. This equatorial undercurrent is stronger than most, with an unusually fast flow of two to three knots – the speed at which portions of the powerful Gulf Stream flow on the surface.

The densest deep water in the ocean lies near the Poles – in the Weddell Sea in the South Atlantic on the borders of Antarctica, and in the North Atlantic near Greenland. Here winds blowing off the ice caps cool the surface water. When this water freezes to form ice packs, the solid substances in it drop down into the unfrozen water below, making this water, which is already cold, even denser and causing it to sink to the bottom.

This dense bottom water flows very slowly away

The current feeds these animals called sea fans. Attached to the seabed, they line up at right angles to the flow, cupping their fronds to capture as much as possible of the food that comes their way. The nearby fish (a relative of the angler fish) faces into the current with the same purpose.

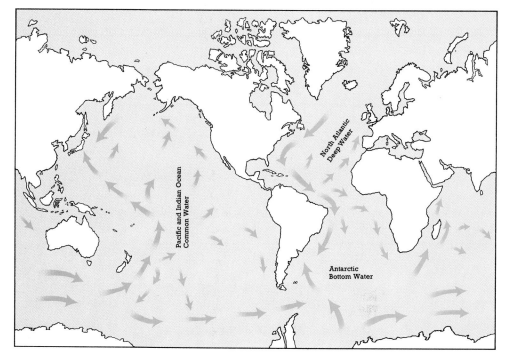

A map (left) of the movement of deep water throughout the oceans, showing the three main types of bottom currents. The schematic north-south section through the Atlantic (below) shows how water sinks in two places: near Greenland in the North Atlantic and in the Weddell Sea in Antarctic waters. This diagram shows how the Antarctic Bottom Water, the densest in the oceans, causes the North Atlantic Deep Water to flow over it where they meet. Along the lighter bands, waters are mixing and therefore altering, both in temperature and salinity.

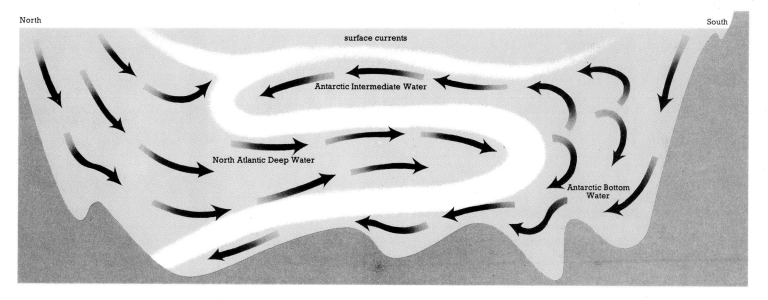

from the two areas in which it was formed, along the western edges of the oceans, where it spreads out to the east and partially mixes with the water above, before returning in much weaker flows to its starting-place. As it flows some of the water in the currents rises very slowly toward the surface, while the rest may stay circulating in the deep ocean for as long as a thousand years. One of these deep currents flowing along the west side of the North Atlantic from the North Pole underlies the Gulf Stream flowing northward along the same coast.

Studying deep currents helps oceanographers to understand the movement of bottom waters in the ocean. We now know that any leakage from dumped containers of radioactive nuclear waste could find its way to the surface some time in the future.

Seas, Climate and Weather

The mist clinging to these Andean peaks is caused by moisture absorbed by air that has moved in from the Pacific, and condensed when it rises over the mountains.

The water needed to irrigate the paddy fields of northeast India is deposited in torrents by the southwest monsoon during the summer months. Without the monsoon, the crops would fail.

Since ocean water changes temperature much more slowly than the air and has a lower annual range of temperature, the oceans affect climate all over the world by warming the atmosphere in the winter and cooling it in the summer. It is a fascinating fact that the upper ten feet or so of the oceans contains as much heat as all the atmosphere over it.

The direction in which a gyre revolves also helps determine the climate in the land areas it passes because the water can carry and lose heat. The climate of Britain and northern Europe, for instance, is very mild compared with that of other countries at the same latitudes (for example, Labrador and Kamchatka), which have temperatures below freezing for most of the winter. This is because of the flow of the Gulf Stream. It begins near Florida with a water temperature of about 73°F. As it moves north it loses heat into cooler water and the atmo-

sphere, but it still carries enough heat via its extension, the North Atlantic Drift, to transport relatively warm water, at about 40°F, into the Norwegian Sea. This keeps Norway's harbors ice free throughout the year and produces much warmer climates in Scandinavia than would be expected normally so far north. By contrast, the coast of Labrador on the other side of the Atlantic, which is farther south than Norway, lies icebound for many months of the year.

The water that warms Scandinavia and Britain continues its journey south by way of the Canary Current. By this time it has lost so much heat that it cools the areas around it, giving the coast of Portugal surprisingly cool waters, before it starts to absorb heat at the Equator.

To the northeast of the Gulf Stream, the Labrador Current carries cold water south along the eastern coast of North America, bringing icebergs with it.

When the warm wet winds over the Gulf Stream and the Sargasso Sea area cross this cooler coastal water, they condense and create fog. Regions with cold coastal waters often have foggy climates.

The variations in day-to-day weather around the world are caused mainly by local prevailing wind patterns that interact with the land or ocean below and are also modified by the ocean currents. The Trade Winds control the climate in the tropics. They begin as cool, dry winds, but as they cross the oceans they absorb heat and moisture, which is lost in very heavy rainstorms over equatorial regions.

The tropical oceans also generate hurricanes, violent tropical revolving storms. Moist air rises

An Apollo 7 photograph reveals the whirling cloud formation of a hurricane close to the Florida Keys.

where the surface waters are very warm, releasing its heat by condensing to form high clouds. This rapidly rising air creates a zone of intense low pressure – the center, or the eye, of the hurricane. Very strong winds revolve around the eye, and can blow down buildings, overturn cars and flatten crops. Hurricanes travel away from the Equator and gradually lose their energy when they pass over land or cooler water.

Life in the Sea

There has been life in the oceans for about 3.5 billion years, and on land for only a fraction of that time – about 400 million years. The plants and animals that are adapted to living on land are generally quite different from those in the sea. For example, trees and shrubs cannot live immersed in seawater, while seaweeds cannot survive for long on land. Birds and mammals (the class of animals that includes humans) are very common on land, but rare in the oceans, although penguins are well-known as a flightless bird that actually lives in the sea, and whales, porpoises and seals are familiar sea mammals. Insects are common on land too – there are about a million species – but there are few types in the sea. While in the atmosphere there is life only in the lowest part – next to the land – the oceans have life at all depths.

At the upper levels, sea life exists in varying degrees of light, which penetrates to a depth of about 600 feet in the open ocean. This is reduced to about 150 feet on the continental shelves, and even less in coastal areas, where the many particles of sediment in the water scatter the light. The lighted area of the ocean is called the photic zone, and below this the water is permanently dark.

Many marine animals do not depend on light – in fact, some have no eyes. Instead, they are often very sensitive to changes in water pressure, and to sound waves which enable them to detect movement that might represent danger, or food, or even a mate.

However, light is essential to almost all plant life, as it provides the energy necessary for photosynthesis, by which plants produce their own nutrients. Therefore, most marine plants can live only in the photic zone. Sea animals feed on these plants or on other animals. The plant-feeding animals must live

where there are plants, so they are also usually limited to the upper parts of the ocean.

There are a very few types of plants that do not make their nutrients by photosynthesis, but by using the chemicals that are produced from hot water springs at the ocean ridge, a process called chemosynthesis. The plants provide food for the animals that live near the ridges, thus creating an oasis of life in the deep sea. Among these animals are varieties of tube-worms that can grow to ten feet or more in length.

The daily change in the ocean's temperature extends only to the top few feet of water, while the greater, seasonal temperature changes extend to a maximum of 600 feet. Below this depth temperature is very stable. The surface temperature of the oceans also varies with latitude – cold in the polar regions, warm near the Equator – but at depths greater than a few thousand feet, there is very little difference in temperature at different latitudes. Because of the low ranges of temperature in their living zones, most marine animals do not have a method of controlling

Animal life in the sea comes in a great variety of forms. The young California sea lions (left) and the bottlenose dolphins (above) are mammals. The beadlet sea anemone (right), the hermit crab (far right) and the violet jellyfish (below right) are also animals, although very much simpler in form than the sea lions and dolphins.

their body temperature – they are cold-blooded.

In the deepest part of the ocean the pressure is more than a thousand times that at the surface. Animals can live under these pressures if they are adapted to them, and most marine animals tend to live within a narrow range of water depth, with a relatively constant temperature and pressure, and not go outside it. For example, deep sea fish, such as rattails, are adapted to the low temperature and high pressure found in the deep. While they can live there successfully, they die if they are brought to shallower waters. Similarly, shallow water fish, such as cod, would die in the deep ocean.

The density of water makes movement in it slow compared to movement in air: fish may swim at about five miles per hour, while some birds can travel at ten times this speed. However, the density of water has the advantage of providing a physical support to marine plants and animals. Thus, the biggest whales, whose skeletons are even larger than dinosaurs', move around easily in the oceans.

The Distribution of Life

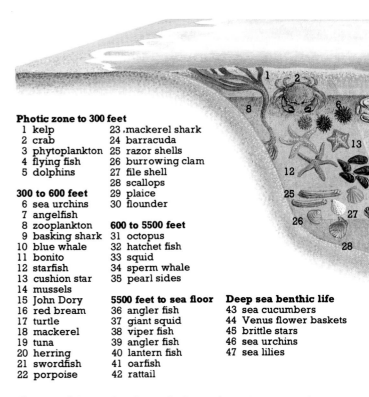

Photic zone to 300 feet
1	kelp	23	mackerel shark
2	crab	24	barracuda
3	phytoplankton	25	razor shells
4	flying fish	26	burrowing clam
5	dolphins	27	file shell
		28	scallops
300 to 600 feet		29	plaice
6	sea urchins	30	flounder
7	angelfish		
8	zooplankton	**600 to 5500 feet**	
9	basking shark	31	octopus
10	blue whale	32	hatchet fish
11	bonito	33	squid
12	starfish	34	sperm whale
13	cushion star	35	pearl sides
14	mussels		
15	John Dory	**5500 feet to sea floor**	**Deep sea benthic life**
16	red bream	36 angler fish	43 sea cucumbers
17	turtle	37 giant squid	44 Venus flower baskets
18	mackerel	38 viper fish	45 brittle stars
19	tuna	39 angler fish	46 sea urchins
20	herring	40 lantern fish	47 sea lilies
21	swordfish	41 oarfish	
22	porpoise	42 rattail	

Some of the animals and plants (not drawn to the same scale) that live at different levels in the sea. They are not all restricted to the levels shown here.

Every part of the ocean has some form of life, even the deepest trenches, and there is a wide variety of life at different latitudes, depths and in different climates. Ocean life can be divided into two types: pelagic life, which lives within the water, and benthic life, which lives on the seabed.

The pelagic environment extends from the shallowest to the deepest waters. It is divided into two provinces: the neritic province, the water over the continental shelf, and the oceanic province, all the water seaward of the shelf break. There are distinct differences in life between these two provinces because of the different conditions in each. The land has a greater influence on the neritic province than on the oceanic province. River water running from the land into the sea reduces the salinity in the neritic region, which varies seasonally, and brings large amounts of nutrients essential for plant growth. Neritic regions are shallow, so most of the water is within the photic zone and may have high seasonal variations in temperature. For these reasons this province is the home of an abundance of life.

In the oceanic region conditions are more stable, and temperature and salinity vary less. Light penetrates farther into this region, as the water is usually clearer. Although the photic zone is only a small percentage of the total area of the oceanic area, it contains most of the life, as it is only here that plants can grow and provide food for the animal life. Below the photic zone, temperature decreases very rapidly with depth, and at depths greater than a few thousand feet temperatures are low and stable. Many small animals move upward from this zone into the photic zone to feed, while other animals rely for food on dead plants and animals falling from shallower water, or prey on other animals.

There are two types of pelagic life: plankton, which drift with the ocean currents, and nekton, which can swim freely. Animals can sometimes belong to both groups – the eggs and larvae of fish are planktonic, but later they start swimming and thus become nektonic. As they have freedom of movement nekton have an advantage over plankton: they can swim to seek food and can try to escape from other animals trying to eat them. Although they can move freely, nekton appear to be restricted to particular areas and depths. Cod, for example, live in the northern Atlantic and Pacific Oceans near the bottom and at depths of less than 1000 feet.

The benthic life of the seabed may be attached to the sea floor, as is the case with coral, or move freely over it, like bottom-living starfish. Still other forms may burrow into the seabed. There are relatively few benthic plants, as only a small part of the sea floor is covered by water shallow enough for photosynthesis to occur.

Benthic animals can obtain food in three main ways. Animals attached to the sea floor are dependent on currents to bring them food, and these creatures, such as oysters, filter suspended particles of food from the water. Fish and other animals that live on the bottom, such as the hermit crab, hunt food, while the animals that live in the sediment eat the remains of dead plants and animals that fall to the sea floor. Benthic animals are very plentiful in the shallow ocean where plants grow, but decrease in numbers with increasing depth and distance from the shore because the food supply is less plentiful.

Different benthic organisms, like pelagic organisms, have certain geographical locations and depth ranges. Some animals, such as mussels, can live between high and low tide level and survive intervals of exposure out of the water. Some animals can only live in water above a certain temperature; for example, barracuda and stingrays would die in water below 54°F. Some, such as the hatchet fish, need the stable conditions of the deep sea, even though it is permanently dark, food is scarce, and the pressure is very high. There are no animals or plants that live over a large range of depths for long periods, although some plankton move vertically hundreds of feet daily, and sperm whales, which spend much of their time at the surface, may dive down more than half a mile below the surface in search of food.

Plankton

A sample of seawater that seems clear and empty of life to the naked eye can show a fascinating variety of plankton when viewed through a microscope. The term plankton comes from the Greek word meaning "to drift," and these tiny organisms float on the surface of the water, or live below the sea surface, or near the seabed. Although some plankton can swim, they are usually so small that they cannot move very fast and are carried along by the ocean currents.

There are two main types of plankton, phytoplankton, which are plants, and zooplankton, which are animals. The phytoplankton need light for photosynthesis, so they are restricted to living in the top few hundred feet of the ocean where light can penetrate. Zooplankton do not need light, as they are animals that feed on plants or other animals, and can live at any depth. However, many zooplankton feed on phytoplankton and therefore are found with them in the upper parts of the ocean. Many zooplankton are the younger stages of larger animals such as fish.

The most common of the phytoplankton are diatoms. These are very small, usually less than a thousandth of an inch in size. Each diatom has a glassy and patterned shell which is in two identical halves, hence the name diatom, meaning "two atoms." Diatoms reproduce by splitting into two, with each split half growing another half to form a new diatom, which will itself split into two. They are particularly abundant in cold waters in the Arctic Ocean and near Antarctica.

Another type of phytoplankton are the coccolithophores, which have very distinctive chalky shells and are also less than a thousandth of an inch in size. Coccolithophores are able to swim by moving a tiny, whip-like hair. They are found mainly in warmer waters and are sometimes so numerous that although they cannot be seen individually they give the sea a milky appearance.

Zooplankton are normally bigger than phytoplankton. Foraminifera are one kind of zooplankton and they range from a thousandth of an inch to many inches in size. They have chalky shells with numerous small holes and this gave them their name, which

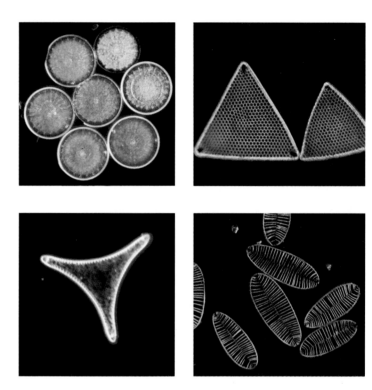

Magnified photographs of the delicate symmetry of four varieties of diatoms. These single-cell plants are phytoplankton. In each of the diatoms shown bottom right the two halves can be seen clearly joined down the middle.

means "hole-bearers." The holes enable the living animal inside the shell to capture and eat food. The shells are often covered with spines. As foraminifera grow they add more chambers to their shells, which often are coiled into spiral patterns.

Radiolarians are another kind of zooplankton, but unlike foraminifera they have a glassy shell, which is very delicate and beautiful and resembles a tiny snowflake. Like foraminifera, they have minute, glassy spines. There are many different types of radiolarians which, like all forms of zooplankton, can be distinguished by their different shells.

How do plankton prevent themselves from sinking to the bottom of the ocean? Plankton are usually very small, so they sink very slowly. The spiky shapes of foraminifera and radiolarians also slow down their rate of sinking. The bodies of some plankton secrete oils or fats which, because they are less dense than seawater, allow the plankton to float. Jellyfish, one of the larger zooplankton, pulsate their bodies as the currents carry them along and this causes them to rise. However, when jellyfish eat, they sink because they relax their bodies in order to trap food under their umbrella-like shapes.

When plankton die, they sink through the water, and although some of them may dissolve or be eaten, the rest fall as a continuous shower of sediment onto the sea floor. The stretches of white cliffs on the southeast coast of England are formed mainly from the shells of coccolithophores, which became sediment about a hundred million years ago; the sea floor subsequently was lifted above sea-level.

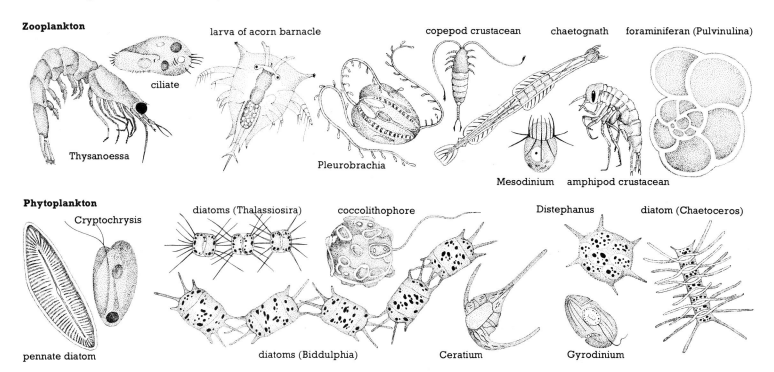

Zooplankton

ciliate

Thysanoessa

larva of acorn barnacle

Pleurobrachia

copepod crustacean

chaetognath

foraminiferan (Pulvinulina)

Mesodinium   amphipod crustacean

Phytoplankton

Cryptochrysis

pennate diatom

diatoms (*Thalassiosira*)

diatoms (*Biddulphia*)

coccolithophore

Ceratium

Distephanus

Gyrodinium

diatom (*Chaetoceros*)

Some typical phytoplankton (above) and zooplankton (top). The examples are drawn to the same scale in each separate row.

The famous white cliffs of England – seen here between Brighton and Eastbourne – are exposed layers of chalk, consisting mainly of fossilized plankton (about 85% coccoliths, 10% foraminifera and 5% other types of plankton and sediment).

Fish

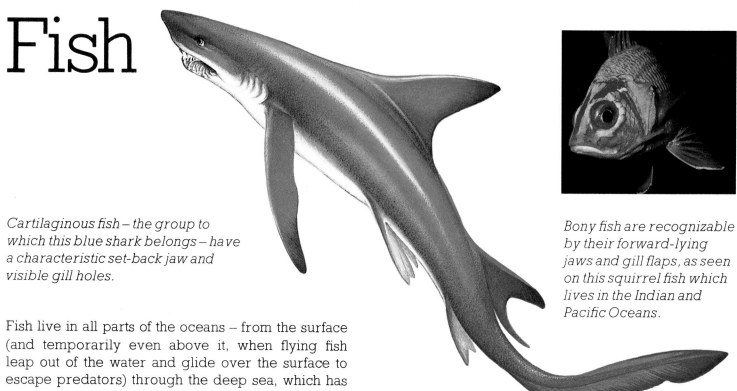

Cartilaginous fish – the group to which this blue shark belongs – have a characteristic set-back jaw and visible gill holes.

Bony fish are recognizable by their forward-lying jaws and gill flaps, as seen on this squirrel fish which lives in the Indian and Pacific Oceans.

Fish live in all parts of the oceans – from the surface (and temporarily even above it, when flying fish leap out of the water and glide over the surface to escape predators) through the deep sea, which has some weird forms of fish, to the bottom itself. There are basically two different types of fish – those that have gristly skeletons of cartilage and those that have skeletons of bone.

Cartilaginous fish have numerous teeth, which are embedded in skin and may be replaced several times throughout their lives. Their skin does not have scales as such but small tooth-like structures called denticles. The teeth and denticles are composed of a hard, bone-like substance. Some cartilaginous fish produce live young, others lay a few yolk-filled eggs, which are often protected by cases. Unlike the bony fish, which have an air-filled swimbladder that keeps them weightless in the water so they can remain motionless without sinking, the cartilaginous fish, without this swimbladder, must keep swimming to avoid sinking.

Sharks and rays are typical cartilaginous fish. Sharks' tails have the upper part of the fin larger than the lower part, so that as the tail moves from side to side the shark moves upward as well as forward. Sharks are among the most feared of creatures. Several of the smaller sharks, such as the hammerhead and the mako, are particularly vicious and hunt smaller fish or eat dead or dying animals; they are also known to attack humans. But the largest sharks, the whale shark and the basking shark, which grow

Some fish have even taken to the air in an adaptation that involved the development of certain fins. This baby flying fish in the Great Barrier Reef was photographed at night.

up to about sixty feet long, feed by filtering small plankton from the water. A smaller shark of fifteen feet, recently discovered off Hawaii, also feeds on plankton. This is the megamouth, so called because of its distinctive gaping jaws.

Rays have very enlarged pectoral fins (those on their sides), and some large rays such as the manta, may grow to a width of twenty feet or more from one fin tip to the other. Rays flap these fins like wings to move through the water. The manta ray feeds on plankton which it swallows in seawater, filtering out the water through its gills and digesting the plankton. Smaller rays such as the skate live on the bottom and have a coloring which is so similar to it that they are

An extraordinary photograph of small marine catfish packing together in a school for protection, taken underwater in Australia's Great Barrier Reef.

well camouflaged; some types can even change their coloration to match different colors of seabed. A few of the rays can be dangerous – the electric ray uses an electric shock to stun its prey, and the stingray has a long tail with a serrated spine which it drives into an enemy.

Bony fish are far greater in number than the cartilaginous fish. Bony fish produce large numbers of eggs, though only a small proportion of them grow to adult fish. Most of the eggs float upward as plankton, and the tiny fish that hatch from them can live for a few days on the yolk in the eggs, but must find food very quickly after that or they will die. Bony fish have a skeleton of bone in their fins as well

as in their bodies. The fins are more flexible than those of cartilaginous fish, too, and can be folded back against the body. Scales (not denticles), that overlap like tiles on a roof, protect their bodies, and their air-filled swimbladders keep them from skinking. Bony fish are much smaller than the large sharks and rays, and except for a few, such as black marlin, rarely exceed ten feet in length.

The bony fish of coral reefs are very highly colored and spectacular. Many are very narrow from side to side, a useful shape for moving through the crevices in coral. They may have specialized jaws for feeding, like the powerful jaws of the parrot fish which crunch the coral skeleton to get to the animals.

In the Deep Sea

The deep sea is permanently dark. The changes between day and night, and between the seasons, have no effect on it. The water temperature in the deep sea is constant and low – about 35°F in the tropical ocean as well as near the Poles – and currents are relatively slow compared with those at the surface.

Down here there is not much food. Most of the dead plant and animal debris sinking from the upper levels is eaten or decays before it reaches the deep sea. Because the amount of food available is very low, there is much less life in the deep sea than there is in shallower areas.

The animals that live on the seabed, the benthic animals, must be able to live with the low food supply and the normally soft sea floor sediment. The animals that live attached to the sea floor and filter fine food particles from the water may have long stalks to raise them off the sea floor away from the bottom sediments that can be stirred up by currents or other animals. Other sea floor animals, such as starfish, sea urchins, and sea cucumbers, get food in a different way. They crawl over the sea floor searching for food, and some of them swallow sediment as they go, then digest the food in it, excreting the rest of the sediment. Many of the animals that crawl over the sea floor leave characteristic trails in the soft sediment which can be recognized on deep sea photographs.

The difficulty of living at great depths has produced a wide variety of strange fish. Deep sea bony fish have a smaller swimbladder, a result of the very

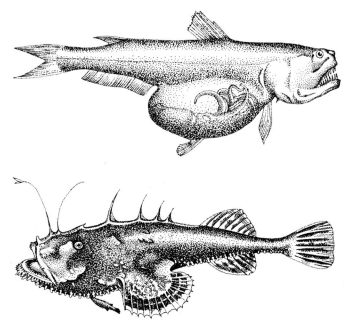

Some specialist adaptations to deep sea life: the male angler fish which attaches itself permanently to the much larger female (top) and the black swallower (above) which can distend its stomach to contain large prey.

high pressures. Some fish do not have eyes, but many can produce their own light. These fish have light-producing organs on their bodies, called photophores, which are arranged in patterns that are different for each type of fish. The light is produced not by the fish themselves, but by a reaction in the photophores of bacteria that live in association

Other deep sea adaptations by animals pictured here include crawling over, skimming or being attached to the ocean floor.

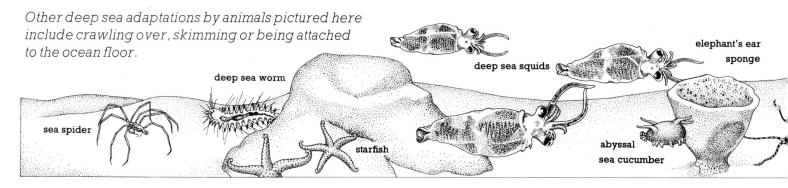

sea spider

deep sea worm

starfish

deep sea squids

elephant's ear sponge

abyssal sea cucumber

The rows of photophores, or light-sources, are clearly visible on the deep sea hatchet fish.

with the fish. The photophores may have complex structures which enable them to be turned on or off. This light may act either as a searchlight to see potential prey, as in the case of lantern fish, or as a lure to attract prey, as in angler fish. The light may help the fish to escape from another predator by dazzling it.

The pattern of photophores can also help a fish to recognize another of the same type to find a mate, as this is a problem in the deep sea where there are very few animals. Some fish solve this problem by living in male-female pairs, although this produces an added problem as the two fish have to compete for food. The angler fish has solved this in a clever way. The male angler fish, which is very much smaller than the female, attaches itself to the female and becomes totally dependent on her for food; even their skins fuse and their bloodstreams connect.

Deep sea fish also have unusual ways of coping with the food shortage. They cut down on their need for food by being small – usually less than a foot long – and light, with small bones. Some have parts of their bodies that act as food lures to other fish, like the lure of the angler fish which dangles in front of its mouth. Deep sea fish are also especially adapted to capture and eat whatever food they find however big it is. Their jaws can open very wide and their stomachs and abdomens can expand enormously to contain animals even bigger than themselves.

Animals grow very slowly in the deep sea because of the low temperature and low food supply, but they also tend to live for a very long time.

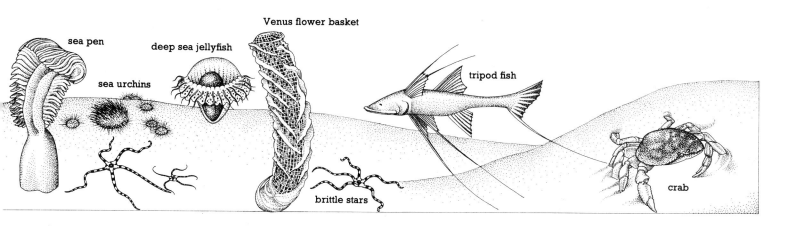

sea pen

deep sea jellyfish

Venus flower basket

sea urchins

tripod fish

brittle stars

crab

Chains of Life

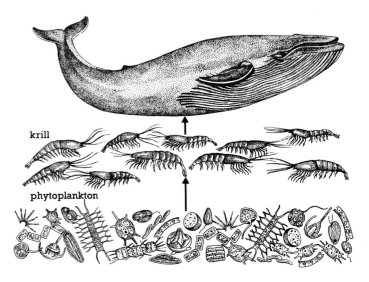

The food chain of the baleen whale

Food chains show the feeding relationships between various plants and animals. There are many food chains in the ocean, just as there are on land. Plants, as we know, are the basis of all life in the ocean, and therefore are the first level of all the food chains there. Seaweeds are abundant around the seashore, but this is a relatively small area, and most of the plants in the ocean are phytoplankton.

Phytoplankton are eaten mainly by some zooplankton that eat only plants. These herbivorous (plant-eating) zooplankton are larger than the phytoplankton, and many of them do not eat just individual plants one by one but swallow large quantities of water from which they filter out the phytoplankton. The photic zone of the oceans is like a phytoplankton soup through which the herbivores move, eating any phytoplankton that they can find. Herbivores must spend most of their life in the photic zone with their food supply.

Zooplankton are much less numerous than phytoplankton. Even though the zooplankton are larger, their total weight, or biomass as it is called, is much less than that of phytoplankton. This is because when zooplankton eat phytoplankton only some of the phytoplankton become part of the zooplankton; the rest is lost as energy or waste.

Herbivores may in turn be eaten by larger animals, the carnivores (animals that eat other animals). As in the link between plants and herbivores, the biomass of the carnivores is less than that of the herbivores they eat. A hundred tons of plants would produce about ten tons of herbivores, which would produce only one ton of carnivores. Because of this, the number of herbivores and carnivores in the oceans must ultimately depend on the number of plants produced.

One of the simpler food chains in the ocean involves the largest animal in the sea, the whale. In the ocean off Antarctica a great many phytoplankton grow in summer because there is a lot of light (the sun remains in the sky for up to 24 hours) and nutrients are abundant. The phytoplankton are eaten by krill, shrimp-like zooplankton up to a few inches long, which form the second level in the chain. Krill in turn are hunted by baleen whales, which filter large quantities of krill out of the water. Whales are the carnivores, at the third level in the food chain.

This is the basic food chain of the baleen whale. However, the food chain that includes the krill and the whale can be more complicated than this and spread out into a food web. Krill are eaten not only by whales, but also by other fish, penguins, and seals. And whales are not always at the end of this food chain, as they may themselves be eaten by other carnivores, such as the killer whale.

Food chains and webs tend to be simpler, with fewer links, when the environment is very changeable, as in the Antarctic, where plants can grow only during the summer and where, as a result, a complex food web does not have time to establish itself. In areas where conditions are stable, where light and temperature do not vary much throughout the year, food webs can be very complex. The food web of coral reefs is extremely complicated and the food webs of the deep sea are also intricate, since conditions there are very stable even though there is not much food.

Fish are in the higher levels of the food chain, and every ton of fish we catch needs at least a hundred tons of plankton to produce it. Although it would be

The murderous hunting equipment of the great white shark's triangular teeth are clearly seen in this shot, taken when the shark – its nose bloodied by the photographer's bait – came to investigate. The great white shark has a complicated food web, shown at right. The lowest level is phytoplankton, leading to the shark seven levels farther on.

more efficient if we could catch and use animals with short food chains or at low levels in a food chain, this would create problems for many animals. For example, if krill were caught instead of whales, the production of food from the ocean could be increased, but they are the essential second level in many food chains; extracting a lot of them from the ocean would disrupt the food chain and affect the lives of animals at higher levels in it.

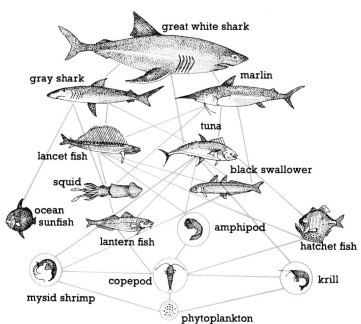

The Largest Animal

Whales are the largest animals that have ever lived on earth. The enormous blue whale, which can grow to a length of over a hundred feet and weigh a hundred and fifty tons, is even larger than the dinosaurs that lived on the earth millions of years ago. Because of their large size, whales have very few enemies, apart from humans.

Whales are among the ocean's mammals – warm-blooded animals that bear live young and suckle them. (Other sea mammals include not only porpoises and seals, but also sea otters, walruses and manatees.) Whales are well insulated from the cold waters of polar seas by a thick layer of oil-rich blubber that lies immediately below the skin and covers the entire body except for the flippers, fin and tail flukes. Whales breathe air through nostrils on the top of their heads, producing a characteristic spout of vapor at the surface when they exhale, by which whaling-ships spot them. Newborn whale calves must swim immediately to the surface of the water to breathe.

There are two groups of whales, the toothed whales and the baleen whales. The sperm whale is the largest toothed whale, reaching a length of sixty feet. It is easily recognizable because of its enormous square head, which contains the spermaceti oil for which it is hunted. The sperm whale dives deeper than other whales, as it feeds on giant squid which live at depths of up to about three thousand feet. Whales can stay submerged for up to an hour at a time by cutting down the oxygenated blood supply to all but essential parts of the body during a dive, and storing oxygen in the muscles and blood as well as in the lungs. Toothed whales have very acute hearing, and produce a sequence of high-frequency clicks, which they use as an echo-locating system for finding their prey, and for judging distances and the speed at which other animals are moving. These clicks might also be a means of communication between whales.

man (6 feet)

dolphin (10 feet)

minke whale (30 feet)

killer whale (30 feet)

humpback whale (50 feet)

sperm whale (60 feet)

sei whale (60 feet)

right whale (65 feet)

fin whale (80 feet)

blue whale (150 feet)

The amazing range of sizes in the whale family, in comparison with the figure of a man. The largest, the blue whale, holds the record for size of all creatures that ever lived on earth.

A right whale's whalebone plates (top) contrasted with a killer whale's teeth (above). The crust on the right whale's head is a chalky excretion. The blow-hole is visible on this beluga whale (left).

Killer whales are smaller than sperm whales, growing to a length of about thirty feet, and can swim very fast. They have very distinctive black and white coloring, somewhat like an enormous porpoise, and a very prominent dorsal fin. Killer whales are not really whales but belong to the same family as dolphins and porpoises. They feed on fish, seals, penguins, and even other whales, and can be very bad tempered and vicious. They have even been known to attack small boats.

The baleen whales are toothless, but have a row of triangular whalebone plates made of a horny material fixed to the roofs of their mouths. In the summer they feed in the polar regions where krill are very abundant, but range widely in the oceans for the rest of the year searching for other krill and plankton. The whale strains the krill from the water by swimming through a shoal with its mouth open, and then closing its jaws and raising its tongue to force water through the plates and out of the sides of the mouth. The krill are trapped on the inner surface of the plates. The largest baleen whale – the blue whale – may gather three tons of krill a day by this method. These whales do not need to swim as fast as the toothed whales, as they do not have to chase their food.

The right whale, the fin whale, the humpback whale, the sei whale, and the minke whale are all baleen whales, and each has distinguishing features. The right whale (so called because it floated when killed and therefore was the "right" whale to catch!) has a very distinctive head shape, with very arched jaws. The humpback whale has a humped back and very long flippers. The fin whale may grow to eighty feet long and the right whale has a maximum length of about sixty-five feet, the humpback can grow to about fifty feet long, the sei to about sixty, and the minke whale to about thirty feet.

Whales have been hunted for many years for their meat, blubber and oil. Several types of whale now are so reduced in numbers that their survival is in danger. We do not have to go on killing whales in such numbers, as there are alternatives for all the products we get from them. Without careful conservation of whale stocks we may lose forever an important food resource and a group of remarkable animals.

Beaches

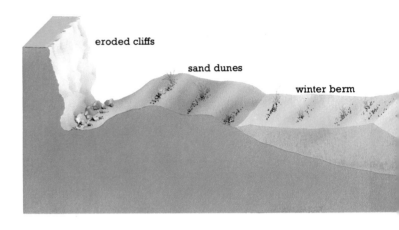

Beaches form wherever more sediment is washed up onto the shore by waves and currents than is washed away. They are relatively young features. When sea-level began to rise about 15,000 years ago at the end of the last glacial period the coastline began to move inward across the continental shelf and only reached its present position about 6000 years ago.

The white shelly beaches of the tropics, the golden sands of temperate regions and the boulder beaches common along stormy coasts are all features of great natural beauty. Sandy beaches are common in sheltered bays, not at the headlands that extend out to sea around the bays. This is because wave action is concentrated at the headlands, breaking them down and washing away the smaller rock fragments. A very narrow beach with large boulders – or no beach at all – is left. The force of the waves is less in the bays, and the waves dump more of their load of rock fragments here, forming a sandy beach.

But not all the sand on beaches comes from the breaking up of headlands and cliffs into fragments. Rivers break up rocks on land to form gravel and sand, which is carried to the sea by the river. This process of the breaking up and removal of rocks is known as erosion. When it reaches the sea this eroded sand can be moved by waves and currents along the coast, where it will be dumped to form sandy beaches. The type of sand on a beach, therefore, shows not only the composition of the local rocks but also that of the inland rocks over which the river has flowed.

The Hawaiian Islands have beaches of black sand, formed from the black lava erupted from the volcanoes on the islands and worn down to sand by the sea and rivers. Beaches may also be formed from shell fragments, producing dazzling white or light-colored beaches. The Bermuda Islands have some pale pink beaches, where the sand is colored with shells of a red foraminiferan, a planktonic animal. Beautiful golden beaches are often found in areas with iron in the rock, which stains the sand particles.

The particles of sand on many beaches are the same size. This is because waves and currents make

Coral sand on a beach in Antigua, one of the Leeward Islands in the Caribbean

the particles rub against each other, grinding them to a regular, smooth shape. The finer pieces of sand that result from the friction are carried out to sea, where they eventually settle as sediment on the continental shelves. Where the waves or currents are very strong, sand may be washed away faster

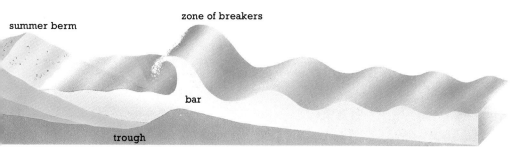

summer berm

zone of breakers

bar

trough

This diagram shows the action of the sea as waves gradually build up banks of finely pounded rock to form a typical sand beach at the edge of an eroded coast.

A black sand beach of volcanic origin on Hawaii Island

A beach consisting of smooth boulders on Little Barrier Island, off the northeast coast of New Zealand

than it is brought in, leaving behind the larger bits of gravel, rock, or boulders. Also, a beach may vary between summer and winter. During the summer there may be wide sandy beaches, but the much stronger winter waves may wash the sand away to deeper water, reducing the width of the beach and sometimes leaving only gravel.

Most beaches have distinctive features that can be easily recognized. Offshore, below low tide level, there may be a longshore bar running parallel to the shore; if there is one, its position can be seen by the waves that break over it. There is a longshore trough between the bar and the beach. This is often the case with barrier beaches, such as those along the east coast of America. The water hurled against the beach by waves does not all return over a bar, but travels parallel to the beach then out through a channel in the bar in a fast rip current. Rip currents running offshore through depressions on a beach or channels in a bar can be dangerous, as they may

carry swimmers out to sea.

The area between the low and high tide levels is called the foreshore, and it slopes gently down toward the ocean. At the top of the shore is a berm, a wide, flat region of the beach above the normal high tide level. Berms are formed by waves that are higher than normal – usually during storms – which deposit sand high up on the beach. A beach may have more than one berm, the highest one being formed during winter storms, and a lower one being formed in the summer and washed away in the winter.

Farther inland from the berms there may be sand dunes, formed of sand that has been blown from the beach by winds coming from the sea. This sand subsequently may be carried even farther inland unless plants and trees start to grow on it. Dunes can protect low-lying areas of land behind them from the sea. In The Netherlands sand dunes are part of the country's defense against flooding from the North Sea.

Estuaries

Estuaries form at the lower reaches of large rivers, where they flow into the sea. Many of the world's major cities – New York City, London, San Francisco, and the like – are built around estuaries because estuaries provided sheltered harbors for ocean-going ships, for trading and transport.

There are three main types of estuaries: those at the lower reaches of rivers, fjords, and lagoons. Since sea-level was lower during the last ice age, with the shoreline near the edge of the present continental shelf, rivers flowed across the shelf to the deep sea. When sea-level rose, it covered the rivers on the continental shelf and estuaries were formed in their present position farther up the old river valleys. Some estuaries, such as the Hudson at New York, have an associated submarine canyon extending part of the way across the continental shelf, marking where the river flowed across the shelf before the sea-level rose. The estuaries are considerably wider than the upper reaches of the river and may be quite deep.

Fjords are estuaries formed in colder regions, where glaciers carved out river valleys during the last ice age. This glacial action modified the typical V-shape of young river valleys, scooping them out into a U-shape, producing narrow, deep, steep-sided fjords. These formations are common in Norway, Scotland, Greenland, Alaska and the Pacific coast of Canada, and the scenery of these areas is very spectacular, with high mountains and almost vertical sides to the fjords.

Lagoon estuaries are wide and shallow. They are usually formed where the flow of the river into the ocean is obstructed by an offshore beach or sandbar. Waves and currents have transported sediment along the coast and deposited it to form an offshore sandbar, usually parallel to the coastline. Storm waves build up the bars until they become barrier islands, which enclose a shallow lagoon. The barriers have narrow channels for the flow of river water and seawater. Lagoons, such as Laguna Madre in Texas, are found

Auerlands Fjord, leading off the great Sognefjord, north of Bergen, Norway – an example of glacial action.

Aerial view, looking north at ebb tide, of the drowned valley of the River Exe, southwest England

on the Gulf and Atlantic coasts of the United States. Another good example is in The Netherlands where the Frisian Islands enclose an enormous lagoon, the Wadden Zee and the Zuider Zee.

In an estuary, freshwater from the river mixes with seawater. Freshwater is less dense than the salty seawater, so it flows out into the ocean on top of the seawater. Besides the flow of river water out of an estuary, seawater flows into and out of the estuary with the tides, coming into an estuary as the tide rises and going out as the tide falls. On the flood tide, when the tide rises, the seawater flows in the opposite direction to the river water, and on the ebb tide, when the tide goes down, they both flow in the same direction. In the open ocean the flood and ebb currents last for the same length of time; but in an estuary, ebb currents last longer than flood currents because of the additional flow of river water.

Estuaries are very useful areas, providing not only harbors, but also large amounts of fish and shellfish, cooling water for power stations, and a dumping-ground for industrial waste and sewage. Sometimes there is conflict between these uses and estuaries become contaminated, killing the plants and animals that are part of the estuary. But with care we can live alongside the plants and animals without destroying their natural environment.

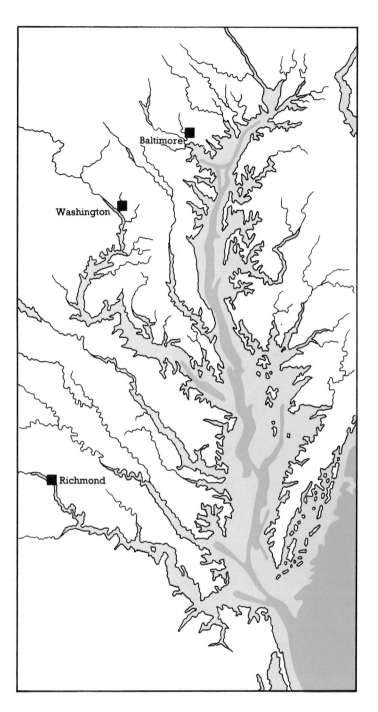

This map shows the wealth of tributaries flowing into the estuary of Chesapeake Bay, another drowned valley.

Deltas

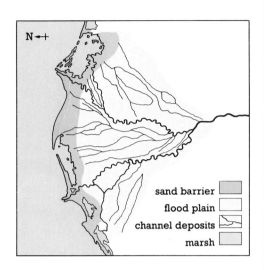

The triangular Nile delta, photographed from Gemini IV, has been gradually extended with soil washed down over thousands of years. The buildup of the delta is shown in the map.

Map legend:
- sand barrier
- flood plain
- channel deposits
- marsh

N

Every river carries sediment, which is deposited where the river water slows, at the river mouth or in an estuary when the river meets the sea. Waves and currents normally move this sediment away from the river mouth and carry it along the coast and deposit it on beaches, on the continental shelf or in the deep ocean. But some large rivers carry more sediment than can be moved away and the sediment accumulates at the river mouth until it forms a delta. Many deltas are triangular in shape, which led to their name, as the fourth letter of the Greek alphabet is delta, a triangle (Δ).

Deltas occur most commonly where rivers that carry large amounts of sediment empty into oceans with small tidal ranges, such as the Gulf of Mexico (Mississippi delta) and the Mediterranean (Nile and Rhone deltas). The weak tidal currents cannot carry away all the sediment dumped at the river mouth. The Mississippi River has formed the largest delta in the

United States because it carries so much sediment – about 300 million tons a year – that the low tidal range cannot shift it all away.

A few rivers, such as the Indus and the Ganges, carry such quantities of sediment that a delta forms even if there is a large tidal range and strong waves. Both these rivers, starting in the Himalayas, carry more sediment than the Mississippi River and, although the tidal range is large where they empty into the Indian Ocean, the rivers have built extensive deltas out into the sea.

Delta formation starts when a river fills its estuary with sediment. Not all large rivers have reached this stage – the Amazon River, with a large estuary and carrying a moderate amount of sediment, is still filling its estuary. After an estuary is filled, sediment begins to accumulate at the river mouth to form the delta proper. As the delta builds up, the river forces channels across it, called distributaries, to allow the

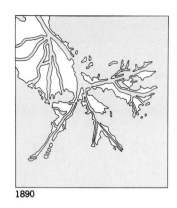

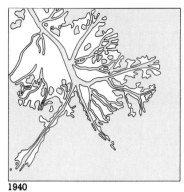

1890   1940

The blue area in this false-color satellite photograph of the Mississippi delta reveals river sediment flowing out into the Gulf of Mexico. (Vegetation on land shows as red patches.) This is a bird's-foot type of delta, and has little sediment filling in the spaces between channels. Changes continue to take place: by 1940 a northeastern channel had formed, while some of the western channels had silted up during the previous fifty years.

river water to flow into the ocean. A distributary is almost the opposite of a river tributary, as it carries water and sediment outward from the main channel to different parts of the delta. Distributaries often extend across the delta from the river in fan-like patterns, giving deltas their characteristic triangular shape. Distributaries continuously build their mouths farther seaward by dumping sediment until the distance to the ocean is so great that the main river cannot keep flowing through these channels and the river shifts its course, forming another distributary. The Mississippi River has changed course many times, leaving a series of abandoned distributaries. As a result, the Mississippi delta has a "bird's-foot" shape, rather than the classic triangular delta shape.

The sandy banks above the water line of distributaries are called levees. They are deposited when the river floods and spills over a distributary. These natural levees rise higher than the areas between distributaries, which are usually lakes or marshes formed by mud being deposited when a distributary overflows its banks.

Deltas are very flat areas, well supplied with freshwater, and are very fertile, as sediment deposited on them by the river during floods provides a continuous supply of rich soil. Because of this, many of the early civilizations prospered on deltas, such as the Egyptian on the Nile. Today deltas are still important as farmland and are also areas of high population. Unfortunately the Nile delta, the site of a magnificent early civilization, is in danger from modern civilization. Since the building of the Aswan High Dam on the Nile River in upper Egypt, much of the sediment that would previously have been carried to the delta is trapped in the lake behind the dam and with no sediment now building up, the Mediterranean Sea is steadily eroding the delta away.

Coral Reefs

Coral reefs are one of the most beautiful and exciting phenomena in the oceans. The coral reef is a biological community consisting of the coral itself and a variety of small animals and plants, of which algae are usually as abundant as the coral. The framework, or base, of the reef is formed by the skeletons of dead coral animals, with the living corals and algae at the top of the reef. As the kinds of reef that grow at sealevel have to be solid enough to withstand the battering of the waves, the framework must be strong. Many fish and other animals and plants live on or in reefs, and all this life forms a rich, varied and colorful community.

Coral reefs occur in warm, tropical oceans where the temperature is higher than 68°F. They need sunlight, so they grow only in clear shallow water down to depths of not much more than a hundred feet. Reefs also need a good circulation of seawater to bring them oxygen and food, so strong wave action is beneficial to them.

Coral is an animal which reproduces very quickly by splitting, to form colonies of coral. Each animal has a chalky skeleton which is joined to neighboring skeletons, forming the strong framework of the reef. In some coral colonies, such as brain coral, it is impossible to see each individual animal; but in other colonies the skeleton of each animal can be seen.

Corals feed on zooplankton. However, the microscopic plants that live within the coral also supply it with food and reef-building materials. The plants in return seem to benefit from the coral, gaining shelter and foodstuffs from it.

There are three main types of coral reefs: the fringing reef, the barrier reef, and the atoll. Conditions on reefs vary from the breaking surf of the open sea edge to the quieter lagoon. The fringing reef grows out from an island, or other land form, but is still attached to it. Coral reefs bordering the Florida Keys, for example, are of this type. A barrier reef is separated from the island or mainland, and may be a few miles distant. The Great Barrier Reef is over a thousand miles long, forming an off-shore breakwater for the east coast of Australia. An atoll is a circular reef surrounding a lagoon, often not associated with any obvious land. Atolls occur mainly in the Pacific and Indian Oceans, rising abruptly from the deep ocean.

A few centuries ago scientists were puzzled to find coral atolls in the deep oceans with no land visible, because they knew that corals could grow only in shallow water. The naturalist Charles Darwin, during his voyage on HMS *Beagle* from 1831 to 1836, examined a number of atolls and put forward a theory for their formation. He suggested that a volcanic island or seamount provided a shallow water base for the growth of a fringing reef. This island would be eroded by the waves and would sink slowly under its own weight. To remain in shallow water, the corals of the reef would grow upward as the island sank until the reef became separated from the island by a doughnut-shaped lagoon, forming a kind of barrier reef. Further sinking of the island below the sea surface would leave only the reef as an atoll, the island being no longer visible.

Darwin's theory was not proved correct until 1952, when holes were drilled into Eniwetok Atoll in the Pacific Ocean. After drilling through almost a mile of coral, the scientists reached the old volcano. It had been sinking for some sixty million years and all this time the coral had been growing upward, keeping pace with the sinking island.

Four stages in the formation of a coral atoll around a volcano, which gradually sank and disappeared after becoming inactive.

active volcano

A typical coral island (top) in the Great Barrier Reef. Wrasse, butterfly and demoiselle fishes (left) and seahorses (above) all live among the coral (center and left).

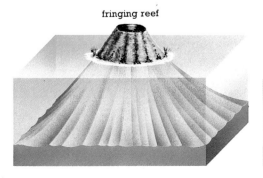

fringing reef

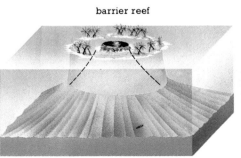

barrier reef

atoll and lagoon

Life on the Shore

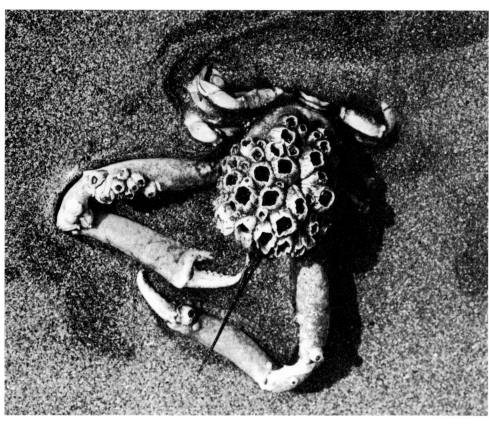

A male masked crab moving on a beach, its shell encrusted with the bases of dead barnacles that once grew there under water and still provide it with some useful camouflage.

The seashore is a difficult environment for the animals and plants that live there. Conditions are constantly changing, and the plants and animals must be adapted in order to survive these changes. Those that live between low and high tide must be capable of living both under water and in the air. They must be able to survive changes of salinity due to rain diluting the seawater, to evaporation, or to tides flowing in and out. The temperature may change drastically, as pools of water warmed by the sun are cooled by the incoming tide. Most difficult of all, they must be able to withstand the force of the waves.

The seaweeds that grow on the seashore are very different from the plants on land. For example, they have no stems, leaves, or flowers; they do not even have roots, absorbing the nutrients they need directly through their cells. They grow abundantly from high tide level down to below tide level, and are most common on rocky shores. Unlike most land plants, seaweeds are not rigid and cannot support themselves, and when exposed to the air at low tide they hang limply over the rocks. Some seaweeds grow attached to the bottom and others float freely in the water. Seaweed provides a hiding-place for many small animals.

Despite the difficult environment, many different types of animals are found on the shore. They protect themselves from their environment in many ways. Some of them have armor – very strong shells that protect them from the battering waves and which also make it difficult for other animals to eat them. A mussel has a pair of shells for protection, and fixes itself to a rock with strong threads. Mussels usually live in large groups and are common in estuaries. Limpets are also armored with a strong shell, and when covered by the tide they crawl over rocks, eating minute plants called algae. At low tide they cling firmly to a rock so that they are not washed away.

Of the marine reptiles, sea snakes very rarely come out of the sea, and the female turtle comes ashore only once a year to lay her eggs. However, the iguanas of the Galápagos Islands spend much of their time on land.

Seashore animals living in sand or mud are prey to shore birds, such as this curlew, plunging its curved beak to reach burrowing clams.

Some of the fauna that live in the tidal margins: a colony of acorn barnacles (below); a mussel (center) attached by its anchor threads, secreted from its foot, which allow it to swing with the current; mussels (right) feeding with their valves wide open.

Some animals burrow into sandy or muddy shores as protection from waves and other animals. Burrowing clams, for instance, burrow into the mud or sand until their shell is hidden, then extend two siphons above the surface to feed. The clam draws in water through the lower siphon, filtering plankton out of the water, and expels the water through the upper siphon. A burrowing clam reacts against being exposed on the surface; if dug up, it quickly tries to hide itself by burrowing. The lugworm, like other worms, is a burrower; it feeds by swallowing sand and digesting the tiny particles of food in it, piling the waste sand on the surface in distinctive casts.

Crabs scavenge on the shore for food, cleaning up dead fish and other animals. Some crabs are good swimmers and search for food on the seabed. Others, such as the sand and masked crabs, burrow and eat food particles in the sand, while still others, such as the small shore crab, live in pools and hide under stones.

This abundance of life along the shore attracts fish into the shallow waters to feed on many of the plants and animals that live on the bottom. Fish, in their turn, are hunted by seabirds – seagulls and the like.

Seawater is Useful

Common salt, which makes up about three per cent of seawater, has been extracted from the oceans for thousands of years. The salt is separated by evaporating the water in the sun. Seawater is piped to large, shallow evaporating-ponds, and the water evaporates, leaving the salt.

Although this common salt (sodium and chlorine) is the most abundant compound dissolved in seawater, other compounds and elements occur in significant quantities. Over half the world's supply of magnesium, a metal used to make light, strong materials for engineering purposes, is extracted from seawater, as is a quarter of the world's supply of bromine, a gas used in the manufacture of gasoline additives.

There are many other elements in seawater but they are not extracted because they are present only in extremely low quantities. It has been estimated that gold has only one part in each thousand billion parts of seawater, so it would be necessary to process tremendous quantities of seawater to extract gold from it, which would make it much too expensive to be economic. However, the total volume of seawater is enormous, about 300 million cubic miles, so the total quantity of gold in seawater is also large – ten million tons. The same is true of many other elements, although at the moment they cannot be extracted economically.

The most useful part of seawater is not the gold and other metals but the water itself. Seawater is the most abundant liquid on earth, and can be converted into virtually limitless supplies of freshwater in dry lands or on islands that are too small to collect enough rainwater. Just as salt has been extracted from seawater, so freshwater has also been extracted from it for thousands of years. One of the earliest reports we have of this is the use of a desalting apparatus by Julius Caesar's army when the Romans were besieging Alexandria, in Egypt, in the first century BC.

Seawater evaporating in salt pans under the Mediterranean sun. The wind-driven pumps on this part of the Syrian coast, near Tripoli, raise the seawater above sea-level onto a level stretch of the mainland, where it evaporates, leaving salt in the pans.

This plant produces magnesia from the magnesium extracted from seawater. Situated on the northeast coast of England, it has an annual capacity of 250,000 tons.

The dry lands that need water are usually very hot, and this heat can be used to extract freshwater from seawater. One method in use today employs heat from the sun to evaporate the pure water from the element-laden seawater inside a large container with a glass roof. At night the roof cools down very quickly and the freshwater condenses. This freshwater runs off the roof and is collected in separate containers.

In some areas the water supply is provided almost entirely by the desalting, or desalination, of seawater.

Kuwait has about fifty desalination plants. Ascension Island in the South Atlantic, which lacks sufficient rainfall to supply its water needs, has about twenty. The town of Key West in Florida also uses seawater to create freshwater. There are about 1500 large desalination plants in the world, each producing 25,000 or more gallons of freshwater each day. The cost of desalinating seawater is generally not too expensive for human or industrial use, but for the irrigation of crops it becomes a very significant factor in the cost of the food produced.

Food from the Sea

plaice

cod

salmon

skate

Four sought-after edible fish from the Atlantic, drawn to the same scale

The oceans supply almost seventy million tons of food a year at the moment, and while this may seem a lot it is only about a twentieth of the total world food supply. People have used the sea as a source of food for a very long time and in some countries it is extremely important – the Eskimo, for instance, relies almost entirely on marine mammals and fish for food. Most of the food from the sea is fish – about ninety per cent. Of this, just six species make up over half the total catches – cod, pollack, mackerel, herring, sardine, and anchovy. The remaining ten per cent consists of whales, crustaceans (crabs, lobsters, and shrimps), mollusks (oysters and clams), and seaweed (kelp).

Although the continental shelves account for only about a tenth of the area of the ocean, about ninety-nine per cent of fish are caught there. The North Atlantic Ocean, the southeast Pacific and the northwest Pacific Ocean produce the highest catches of fish. The oldest large-scale fisheries are in the North Atlantic, where haddock, herring, cod, plaice, sardine, and mackerel are caught. Many of these fisheries have been overfished, resulting in a fall in the numbers of fish in the oceans – as well as declining catches. Japan is the major fishing nation in the northwest Pacific, catching mainly squid, anchovy, and mackerel. The Peruvian fishery in the southeast Pacific Ocean yields chiefly anchovy and is one of the largest fisheries in the world, catching up to ten million tons a year. Anchovy eat phytoplankton, so they have a very short, one-step food chain, which makes them abundant where there is a good supply of phytoplankton, as there is off Peru.

The method of catching fish depends on where in the ocean the fish live. Commonly, bottom-living fish are caught commercially by a bottom trawl, which is hauled slowly along the seabed by ships called trawlers. Where the bottom is too deep or too rough for trawling, long lines with hooks are used. Pelagic fish that swim in large schools, or shoals, are caught with mid-water trawls, or drift nets, which are laid out around a shoal of fish and then hauled in. Whales are hunted by small vessels called catcher ships. When a whale comes up to the surface to breathe, it is killed by a gun-fired harpoon with an explosive head. The carcass has air pumped into it to keep it afloat and it is then towed to a factory ship, which reduces the mammal to whale meat, oil, and bone meal. Many catcher ships work with each factory ship. Whaling has become so mechanized and intense in the last thirty years that many species of whales are so heavily overfished that they are near extinction.

Besides hunting for food from the sea, it is also possible to farm the sea, raising animals in protected environments that are especially suited to nurturing particular species. Oysters, clams, and shrimp are mainly farmed. One oyster produces millions of eggs when it spawns, and the eggs soon develop into larvae, which are free-swimming. The larvae attach themselves to any hard surface and develop into small oysters, called "spat" because oystermen once believed that adult oysters spat them out. The oyster

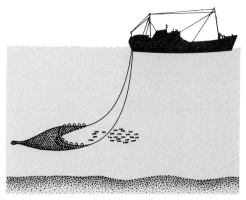

A mid-water trawl is employed for catching pelagic fish, such as herring and mackerel. To keep its mouth open, the top leading edge is lined with floats and the bottom one is weighted. The length of tow line controls the depth of the trawl.

Portuguese fishwives at Sesimbra, south of Lisbon, marketing a fresh catch from the Atlantic fisheries

farmer distributes bits of old oyster shells or roof tiles in the ocean and collects them when oyster spat has settled on them; he uses them to form new oyster beds in the shallow waters of bays or estuaries. The farmer clears the area of any animals that will eat oysters, such as starfish, and places the oysters in their new home, where they are allowed to grow. They may be supported on wooden racks or suspended on wires.

Oysters feed by filtering small plants and animals out of the water they pump in and out of their digestive cavities. To grow, they need a constant supply of water and protection from predators. Unlike a farmer on land, who must carry food to his animals or let them freely graze, the oyster farmer can leave the feeding to the sea. Its currents and tides bring food to the oysters, and the farmer then harvests the crop.

Power from the Sea

The sea has vast amounts of energy in its tides, waves, and currents. People who live on coasts have been using the rise and fall of the tides to turn paddlewheels in tidal mills for centuries. Tidal mills are recorded in England as early as the eleventh century in the Domesday Book, a list of land ownership made by William the Conqueror. Settlers brought their knowledge of tidal mills to America, and there was such a mill grinding corn near Boston in the seventeenth century. The tidal mills trapped water in an estuary at high tide and then released the water at low tide through a narrow channel where it turned a water wheel.

The power available from tides depends on the tidal range. The lower the tidal range, the larger the volume of water that is needed and the larger the turbine. And for modern mills geared for major industrial uses, only areas with a range greater than about fifteen feet are suitable. Only a few areas in the world have such a high tidal range, and these include the coast of British Columbia and the Bay of Fundy in North America, the west coast of England, and the northwest coast of France. The method of producing electricity from the tides is similar to that used on hydroelectric plants on rivers, in which water flows from a higher to a lower level and turns a turbine.

Tidal power is more difficult to generate than river power because the water flows in opposite directions at flood tide and ebb tide. Power production in tidal plants is controlled by the tidal cycle, either a daily or semi-daily cycle, so the power produced will vary throughout the day unless there is some way of storing the power generated until it is wanted.

The Rance estuary, on the coast of northwest France, has the world's only large-scale tidal power station. The Rance has a tidal range of over forty feet at spring tides. The water level is controlled by a dam at the mouth of the estuary. Turbines are contained in tunnels in the dam below the waterline and these turbines can be driven by water flowing into the estuary as well as out of it. Shipping can still travel in the estuary through lock gates at one side of the dam. The Rance tidal power station cost $100 million to build, an enormous amount of money, although less than a nuclear power station would cost.

Waves are another source of energy from the sea.

In 1701 a tide-powered water pump was installed under London Bridge. We can see one of its wheels in this engraving made nearly fifty years later. "W" marks the winch handle used to engage gears and raise or lower the wheel and change its direction according to the tide.

An aerial view of the Rance tidal power station in northwestern France, which has an annual generating capacity of 608,000,000 kilowatt hours. Its turbines lie in tunnels below the sector stretching from the center of the dam to the farther shore. Sluice gates between the nearer shore and the artificial island allow the water on both sides to be held at equal levels.

The total amount of energy in waves is much greater than that in tides. A single wave six feet high in water thirty feet deep has a power of about three kilowatts for each foot of the wave, enough to run an electric fan if it could be extracted. Areas like the west coast of Britain have an almost continuous supply of suitable waves, but it is difficult to convert the energy of waves into electricity. A wave power converter in the form of a string of large, floating vanes has been proposed. The vanes would rock up and down with the waves, driving water past turbines and so producing electricity. But no full-scale systems such as this yet operate.

Tide and wave power have one advantage over other forms of power: they will not run out. The world's reserves of oil, gas, and coal are limited, but the tides, which get their energy from the gravitational attraction of the moon and sun on the earth, and waves, which get energy from the wind, should last forever.

Offshore Oil and Gas

About a quarter of the world's oil and gas now comes from beneath the oceans, and there may be as much oil in off-shore areas as there ever has been on land.

Oil and natural gas are formed from the remains of plants and animals that lived in water – in rivers, lakes, or the sea – and which settled to the bottom when they died. The plant and animal remains could only form oil or gas where there was not enough oxygen to destroy them and if sediment buried them. As the remains were buried and then decomposed, heat and pressure slowly changed them to oil and gas. This process took a very long time, at least a few million years.

Deltas are rich in plant and animal life, with abundant sediment, favoring the formation of oil and gas. In the oceans, oil and gas are found at continental margins, as there is plenty of life, and thick sediments, in these areas. Conditions in the deep ocean are not suitable for oil and gas formation, since fewer plants and animals live there, and most of them are destroyed before they reach the ocean floor, where the sediment is much thinner.

Oil and gas are lighter than the surrounding rocks, and after formation they tend to move into rock that is porous enough to hold the oil and gas, such as sandstone or limestone, known as reservoir rock. Solid, or impermeable, rock such as shale caps this reservoir and stops the oil and gas from rising upward and escaping to the surface. The search for oil and gas is a search for suitable reservoirs, which are detected by seismic profiling, a much more powerful form of echo-sounding which can detect the rock structure hidden beneath the ocean floor. Seismic profiling can find rocks that hold the promise of having the right properties and structure to be reservoirs, but there is only one way to find out whether they definitely contain gas or oil and that is by drilling into them.

The first offshore oil well was drilled as long ago as 1896 off the coast of California, but the early drilling rigs could only work in shallow waters. In 1953 the first jack-up rig was built, and this could work in deeper water of up to about 300 feet by lowering legs down onto the seabed then jacking the drilling-platform up above the sea surface, out of reach of the waves. Semi-submersible rigs were developed in 1962 to work in even deeper water. These do not rest on the seabed but have large buoyant floats which are submerged and support the platform above the sea surface. The semi-submersible is moored in position. Drilling-ships are the most recent type of drilling-rig. They are not attached to the seabed at all; instead they keep in position using propellers around the hull that can move the ship in any direction and thus keep it stationary relative to the ocean floor, despite strong currents and storms. Drilling a well in deep water is very expensive, costing many millions of dollars, and is a gamble as many drill sites yield only water or uneconomic quantities of oil or gas.

If the drilling-rig finds oil or gas, a production platform is used to extract it. Production platforms stand on the seabed, and in deep water they can be enormous structures. In the North Sea there are platforms in water 500 feet deep, and off California they are working in more than 1000 feet of water.

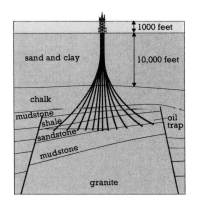

This typical drilling profile of an offshore rig shows oil being tapped nearly twenty times as far below the sea floor as the depth of water in which the rig is standing.

A symbol of humanity's newest conquest of the sea: the space-age majesty of a production platform, standing in 500 feet of water, dominates the North Sea.

Mining the Sea Floor

Oil and gas come from under the ocean floor, but there are also useful resources to be found on the seabed. Mining under water is more difficult and more expensive than mining on land, so if there is an adequate supply of a mineral on land it is not usually economic to mine it under the sea.

The most useful mineral deposits are those in the sediments that have come from the land which are found in the shallow waters of the continental shelves. The most valuable of these are sands and gravels, which occur extensively on the shelf and are easily mined by dredging. Sand and gravel are used in vast quantities for building; Britain alone uses about a hundred million tons of sand and gravel each year, of which about ten million tons comes from the sea bed. Major deposits of shells, such as those in the Bahamas, are also mined in large quantities as a source of lime, which is used for agriculture or in cement.

Metals are heavier than other rock fragments, and this leads to their concentration on the seabed. Rain and wind weather the metal ore on land, and rivers then carry it into the sea. Waves, tides, and currents sort the rock fragments, and the heavier particles settle out of the water first, forming metal-rich sands called placer deposits. These are typically beach deposits, but as sea-level has changed many times and the shoreline has moved across the continental shelf, many placer deposits are now found on the continental shelves. Placer deposits may also be old stream deposits, the metals concentrated by the action of the flowing water which removed the lighter rock. Like sand and gravel, placer deposits can be mined by dredging. Diamonds have been obtained from placer deposits mined off the coast of Africa, gold from placer deposits in Alaska and the west coast of Canada, tin from southeast Asia, and titanium and zirconium from the coast of Australia.

The deep ocean floor has a completely different type of mineral deposit, commonly called manganese nodules. These are rounded and blackish and about an inch in diameter. They occur in all the oceans, and are sometimes abundant enough to cover the seabed.

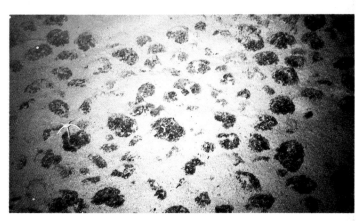

Piles of tun shells (top) awaiting export from the Philippines, the center of the shelling industry. This is how manganese nodules (above) appear on the Pacific floor in the underwater prospector's searchlight.

Manganese nodules are formed from substances dissolved in seawater, and usually grow in layers around shells in the sediment. Although composed mainly of manganese and iron, they are valuable for the smaller amounts in them of copper, nickel, and cobalt, minerals that are in particularly heavy demand. Nodules with the highest concentrations of these metals occur in the northeast equatorial Pacific.

Mining manganese nodules in the deep ocean, in water depths of a few miles, is much more difficult than mining them on the shallow continental shelf. Many companies have experimented with mining nodules, trying out different ways of lifting them to the sea surface. One way is to lay a pipe to the sea bed and to suck the nodules up the pipe. Another way is to lower buckets to the seabed in a continuous chain and scoop up the nodules. But all the methods need especially designed ships and complicated equipment. At the moment the minerals in manganese nodules are being mined on land, but when our land deposits run out there is a vast resource on the ocean floor.

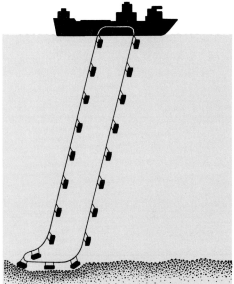

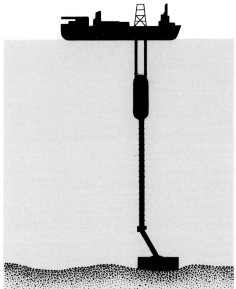

It would be possible to dredge manganese nodules either by bucket chain (top) or by a suction trailer (above), similar to the one (left) coming to the surface alongside its parent hopper.

Navigation

Oceanographers depend on accurate navigation, the method sailors use to determine the positions of ships at sea. Without it, measurements of currents and water depth, temperature and other characteristics of the ocean would be meaningless.

Ships describe their position in terms of latitude and longitude. Latitude is the angle – taken from the exact center of the earth – between the Equator and the position being measured. It is given in degrees north or south of the Equator, ranging from 0° at the Equator to 90° at the Poles. Each degree is divided into sixty minutes. The latitude of New York City, for example, would be stated as forty degrees, forty-five minutes north (40°45'N). Points on the earth's surface having the same latitude lie along imaginary circles parallel to the Equator called parallels. The 49°N parallel, for example, forms much of the boundary between the United States and Canada.

Imaginary circles running north–south through the Poles of the earth are called meridians. The longitude of a point on the earth is the angle between the Meridian it is on, the center of the earth, and the Greenwich meridian which passes through the Royal Observatory at Greenwich near London. Points on the Greenwich Meridian are said to have a longitude of 0°, points to the east and west of it have longitudes up to 180°. As with latitudes, each degree is divided

This eighteenth-century sextant is a fine example of the optical instruments used by the masters of sailing ships for finding their position at sea.

into sixty minutes. New York City has a longitude of 73°59'W; Moscow 37°42'E.

Distance and speed at sea are also related to latitude and longitude. A nautical mile is 6076 feet, the distance between points one minute of latitude apart along a meridian. A ship traveling at one nautical mile per hour is said to be moving at a speed of one knot. The term "knot" comes from the way ships measured their speed before they had modern equipment. Sailors tied a piece of wood, or log, to the end of a piece of rope that had knots in it at regular intervals and threw the rope overboard. As the ship moved away, they calculated its speed by counting the number of knots that passed overboard in a given

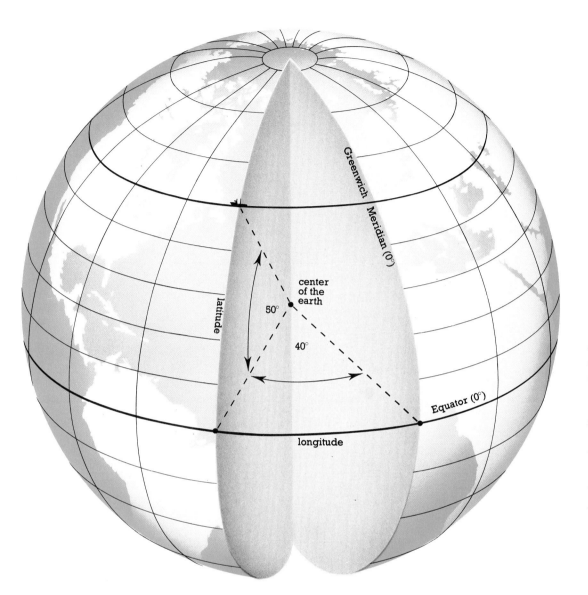

A diagram of the globe, cut open along the Greenwich Meridian. This displays the principles by which the degrees of angle for latitude and longitude are calculated. If a ship's navigator were taking this position at the edge of the continental shelf northeast of Newfoundland, he would read it as 50° north, 40° west.

period of time. Ships now use more accurate methods for measuring their speed, but the device that measures it is still called a log, and speed is still expressed in terms of knots.

In other ways, too, navigation during earlier centuries was more an art than a science. The traditional method for determining latitude and longitude at sea is called celestial navigation. The essentials of this method involved measuring the angle between the horizon and the sun, moon, planets or stars and making a calculation with this and the time of day or night. The result enabled the ship's position to be plotted on a chart. Sailors relied on celestial navigation for hundreds of years, but it

was not very accurate and could not be used in cloudy weather. Many modern sailors in small boats still use this method. However, today most ships employ electronic equipment for navigation. The ship picks up radio signals transmitted by a number of stations on land or from satellites in orbit. As a satellite traveling a known path passes overhead, the ship's navigator can determine first how far he is from the satellite and then the exact time when the distance is shortest between the ship and the satellite; then he can use this to calculate the position of the ship in relation to the known position of the satellite at the given hour.

Charts

Before the oceans were charted, sea travel was hazardous and ships frequently foundered. Sailors could not be sure of the depth of the water in which they planned to sail, nor did they know what dangers lurked beneath the surface. By the end of the last century, however, charts showing depth and hazards, as well as shorelines, landmarks, and positions of lighthouses, had been compiled for most major sea lanes. All ships rely on them today.

To be absolutely accurate, marine charts, like maps, would have to be spherical like the earth itself. In practice, however, charts are flat and give a distorted view of the earth's curved surface. They are produced by projecting the imaginary grid system of parallels and meridians that encircles the earth onto a flat surface.

Map and chart makers have devised various ways to do this. One of the best known is the Mercator projection, named after the sixteenth-century Flemish geographer Gerardus Mercator who devised it. Mercator imagined a light at the center of the earth casting the earth's grid lines as shadows on a cylinder wrapped around the earth. This cylinder, unrolled, is the basis of Mercator projection maps and charts. Features at the Equator are undistorted, but towards the Poles, oceans and land appear much bigger than they really are because they are farther from the light and their shadows are therefore larger. On a Mercator projection map, for example, Greenland appears to be about the size of the United States, although it is actually much smaller in size.

On older marine charts, depths of water, or soundings, were given in fathoms. A fathom is six feet, the approximate length of line a man could hold between his hands with his arms outstretched. The measurements came from sailors who attached a piece of lead to a line adorned by knots or cloth streamers every six feet, threw it overboard and payed out the line until the lead reached the bottom. Then they measured the line. When the water was deeper than the length of line available, they called the depth "unfathomable."

The lead and line method also provided informa-

tion about the sea floor, especially when tallow, a type of fat, placed in a hole in the lead picked up a sample of the bottom. And this information too was indicated on some marine charts in notations such as rky (rocky), Sh (shells), S (sand) and Co (coral). These notations are still used on marine charts. Today echo sounding provides a more accurate profile of the sea floor than the old lead and line method.

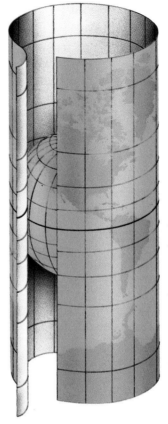

The principle used in making a Mercator's projection of the earth's surface is graphically demonstrated by these two figures. The resulting distortion of distances in the Arctic and Antarctic regions (they are much too large in relation to the rest of the globe) is very obvious.

A typical marine chart as currently used by seamen. The scale of the actual chart, showing waters north of Boston, Mass., is 1:25,000, and it has been retained in this reproduction. The inset photograph shows a ship's officer plotting his position with the aid of such a chart.

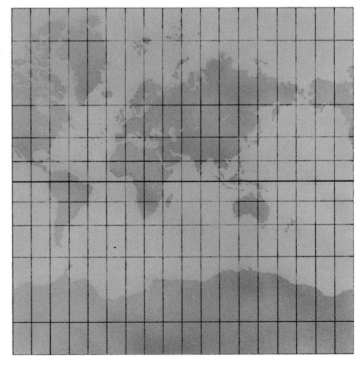

The Law of the Sea

Freedom of the seas is an age-old concept, but it has been challenged for centuries. One of the first declarations on the ownership of the oceans was made by the Pope in 1493. He divided the oceans between Spain and Portugal, the two major sea powers at that time, giving them the exclusive right to trade with the East and West Indies. This could last only as long as Spain and Portugal had the power to enforce it, and it was lost by 1588 when the Spanish Armada was defeated by England.

In the eighteenth century the width of the territorial sea was determined to be three miles — about the distance a country could defend with cannon fired from the shore. The high seas, the area outside the territorial sea, were considered free to all countries. This custom among nations continued until about thirty years ago, when our knowledge of the oceans and technical advances made it possible to exploit offshore mineral deposits and to fish certain grounds more efficiently.

As a result, nations have been reaching farther and farther away from shore for their resources, producing many claims to the oceans. For example, in 1947 Peru claimed ownership of the ocean for 200 miles from shore – a distance that included the all-impor-

An ugly incident at sea during the international dispute over territorial waters that was called the "Cod Wars." The British frigate Naiad *is seen here in collision with the Icelandic gunboat* Tyr *in 1976. The Icelander, towing a warp-cutting device, was trying to get between the British trawler in the background and its nets.*

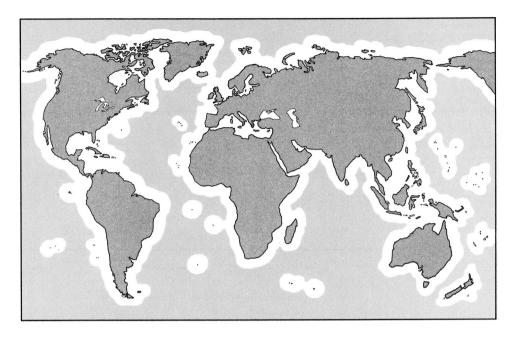

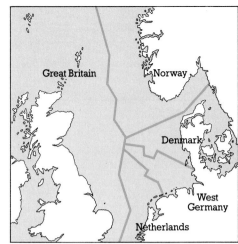

The share-out of the oil-rich North Sea bed as finally negotiated between the neighboring states.

This map shows the general extent of the 200-mile exclusive economic zone that has been proposed by a UN conference.

tant economic reward of the anchovy catch for Peruvian fishermen. In subsequent years, other countries extended the traditional three-mile limit to varying widths from twelve miles up to 200.

Issues about who should have what were brought into sharpest focus over mining the sea floor, chiefly for oil, gas, and manganese nodules. In 1945 President Harry S. Truman announced that the United States owned the "natural resources of the subsoil and sea bed of the continental shelf beneath the high seas but contiguous to the coast." Sparked by this and by the awareness that existing laws were inadequate, the United Nations began to prepare for an all-embracing Conference on the Law of the Sea. At the first Conference, held in Geneva in 1958, delegates drew up four conventions. These dealt with territorial seas and their contiguous zones, the high seas, fishing and the conservation of living resources, and the continental shelf. Unfortunately, the conventions became insufficient to legislate on problems arising from the developing uses of the oceans. A further two conferences were held, the last of which continued over seven years. During the lengthy negotiations, concern was voiced over the

technology of the huge Russian and Japanese fleets that enables them to overfish whole areas of the sea. Heated arguments developed between the industrialized and the developing nations over the right to mine the seabed. And even while the conferences were being held confrontations occurred when some countries such as Iceland and Ecuador tried to physically prevent foreign ships from fishing within their proclaimed 200-mile fishing zones.

While at times a resolution seemed impossible, broad agreement was finally reached in 1980, although this draft treaty has not been ratified. According to the 1980 draft treaty, the accepted limit for territorial seas is twelve miles. There is also a 200-mile exclusive economic zone, the EEZ for short. Coastal nations have the right to exploit all the marine resources in their EEZs. This means that each nation can prevent other countries from fishing and mining in its EEZ, although they may sell rights to other nations.

As for the freedom of the seas, the treaty upholds the right of innocent passage on both the high seas and within the twelve-mile limit, including passage through straits lying within a territorial sea.

The Future of the Sea

We used to think that the seas had unlimited resources and could not be overfished or damaged. Until this century this was true, so long as the human population of the world was still low and technical limitations restricted our use of the oceans. This has now changed, as the population has increased rapidly and there have been major technical advances allowing us to exploit the oceans more extensively.

Fishing has become a mechanized, large-scale operation to supply the great quantities of food needed by an expanding population. The world fish catch increased at about seven per cent each year after 1945 until it had reached fifty million tons by the late 1960s. This intensive fishing so reduced the fish stocks that they could not regenerate fast enough and many important fisheries collapsed – such as the herring fishery in northwest Europe after 1974. Many species of whales have also been hunted almost to the point of extinction. The oceans could supply much of the food requirements of the world in the future, but only if fisheries are managed carefully and we learn to recognize that a species of fish is not an isolated population but part of a food chain, and interference with any part of that chain can lead to falling stocks of the fish we need.

The greatest threat to the future of the oceans, especially the coastal zone, is pollution. The oceans are still used as a dumping ground for waste, in many cases with serious consequences. Much of the sewage from coastal cities is discharged directly into the ocean. Sewage contains nutrients (such as phosphates and nitrates) that are good for marine plants, so it can be beneficial to the oceans and may be thought of as food for marine life instead of pollution, a partial repayment for the vast quantities of food taken from the ocean. However, this will only work if the amount of sewage discharged into the ocean is carefully controlled, as too much sewage reduces the oxygen content of the seawater, depriving animals of oxygen and leading to their death.

One of the most spectacular forms of pollution comes from oil spills, by the wrecking of oil tankers, or blow-outs from offshore drilling-platforms. The blow-out on the Ekofisk Bravo rig in the North Sea in 1977 released about 4000 tons of oil a day for over a week, producing an oil slick covering over 2500 square miles. Oil is harmful to most plants and animals and spoils beaches. Manufactured chemicals are also likely to cause damage to the oceans. Pesticides such as DDT get washed into the oceans and are concentrated in marine animals. There is evidence of reproductive failure in birds that feed on them. Chemicals can also be transmitted to the oceans by the atmosphere, and the quantity of lead in the oceans is increasing rapidly due to the use of lead in gasoline which is released into the atmosphere. Nuclear explosions, too, have released radioactive particles into the oceans. Some countries even discharge low-level nuclear waste into the oceans.

Human deaths have been attributed to man-made pollution in the oceans. Between 1953 and 1970 in Japan 111 people died or became severely ill, and this was found to be caused by mercury poisoning. Chemical processing plants had released mercury into Minamata Bay, where it was absorbed by fish and shellfish, which were eaten by the victims.

The oceans are a challenge. Our present knowledge of the oceans is still inadequate, but if nations can work together to learn about control, and manage the oceans, the oceans will survive and play a vital part in the future of mankind.

In the sea off St Croix in the Virgin Islands a SCUBA-diving engineer tests progress on a revolutionary new underwater structure. This is one of many projects that have been designed by scientists, architects and engineers in different parts of the world to realize a dream of the future – that of utilizing the seabed both for food production and as a human environment. The University of Texas experiment shown here is based on the principle that running a low electric current through wire mesh underwater causes a hard incrustation to settle on the wire, making it as strong as concrete.

Glossary

Abyssal plain: the very large, flat floor of the deep sea

Benthos: plants and animals living on or very near the sea floor

Carnivore: an animal that eats other animals

Chlorophyll: a green coloring-matter that is found in all green plants and is needed for photosynthesis

Crust: the outer layer of the earth, extending on the average to about four miles below the sea floor in the oceans and about twenty miles below continents

Current: a continuous flow of seawater

Delta: an accumulation of sediment at the mouth of a river

Ebb tide: a falling tide that causes an outgoing, or ebb, current

Echo-sounding: measuring the depth of the oceans using sound-waves to reflect from the sea floor; the interval between sending and receiving the sound-wave gives the depth

Element: a simple substance, such as oxygen or sodium, that cannot be broken down any further by chemical means

Estuary: an inlet of the sea at the mouth of a river where freshwater dilutes seawater

Fathom: a nautical measurement of water depth, equal to six feet

Flood tide: a rising tide that causes an incoming, or flood, current

Food chain: the sequence in which each organism in the ocean is the food for another

Fracture zone: long, linear features of the sea floor that divide ocean ridges into segments; they may be thousands of miles long

Guyot: a flat-topped seamount

Gyre: a pattern of currents that moves water around the ocean in a circle

Herbivore: an animal that eats only plants

Knot: a speed of one nautical mile per hour

Lagoon: a body of water separated from the open sea by sand bars or coral reefs

Latitude: distance north or south of the Equator of a given position, measured in degrees; the Equator has a latitude of 0°, the North Pole 90°N and the South Pole 90°S

Log: a device for measuring the speed of a ship

Longitude: a measurement of distance given in degrees east (to 180°E) or west (to 180°W) from the Greenwich Meridian (0°)

Mantle: the layer of the earth beneath the crust. It starts at depths of about 3 miles below the ocean floor and at 20 miles beneath continents.

Meridian: an imaginary circle on the earth's surface passing through the North and South Poles, and used as a base for measuring east-west distances

Mineral: a naturally occurring substance with a fixed chemical composition

Nautical mile: a distance of 6076 feet

Navigation: the process by which mariners plot the positions of ships at sea and guide ships around the oceans

Neap tide: a tide that occurs at the moon's first or third quarter when the sun's gravitational influence is working primarily against the moon's so that the tidal range is low

Nekton: free-swimming animals

Nutrient: an element necessary for plants to produce organic matter

Ooze: a fine-grained, soft, deep ocean sediment composed of the remains of dead plants and animals

Parallel: an imaginary circle on the earth's surface parallel to the Equator and joining points of equal latitude

Pelagic: open ocean, as in pelagic plants and animals that live away from the ocean floor; pelagic sediments are those that fall to the sea floor from the waters above

Photic zone: the zone of the ocean into which light penetrates

Photophore: the light-producing organ of deep sea fish

Photosynthesis: the process by which plants convert energy from the sun, with the aid of chlorophyll, carbon dioxide, and water, to produce carbohydrates, the source of all food

Phytoplankton: floating or drifting microscopic plants

Plankton: plants and animals that float or drift in the oceans

Plate: one of the rigid areas which together make up the earth's outer surface. Plates move on less rigid rock beneath them, and are in movement in relation to each other

Precipitation: the depositing of water onto the earth's surface as a solid (snow and hail) or liquid (rain and dew)

Salinity: a measurement of the amount of dissolved elements in seawater

SCUBA: Self-Contained Underwater Breathing Apparatus

Seamount: an ocean floor volcano, active or inactive, that sometimes extends above the sea surface. The term can also be used for any solitary peak in a ridge.

Sediment: a deposit formed from rock particles or animal remains

Sonar: the use of sound waves to detect underwater objects, such as schools of fish

Sounding: the depth of water at any point

Spring tide: the tide that occurs at new or full moon when the gravitational influence of the sun is working primarily in line with the moon, so that the tidal range is high

Submersible: an underwater vessel used to carry people to the ocean deeps

Tide: the rise and fall of sea-level once or twice a day caused by the pull of gravity of the sun and moon

Tsunami: the Japanese word used in oceanography for a wave caused by an undersea earthquake or volcano

Turbidity current: a powerful current, carrying mixtures of fine sediment particles, that travels down the continental slope to the abyssal plain

Water pressure: the weight or density of seawater on an object; it increases with greater depth

Zooplankton: floating or drifting animals

Index

Credits

The Publishers gratefully acknowledge
permission to reproduce the following
illustrations:

Aerofilms Limited 11, 40, 69tl; Heather Angel 27br,
67r, 74, 75br, bc, 84t; Ardea London 19 (I. Beames),
58, 63 (V. Taylor), 75t (J. & S. Bottomley); Barnaby's
Picture Library 12, 41, 70, 76; S. Summerhays/
Biofotos 59, 73tr; Ian Took/Biofotos 16; BBC Copyright
Photographs 15, 20, 22, 25; British Petroleum 34;
J. Allan Cash Limited 50l, 57, 68; Bruce Coleman
Limited 52, 53, 67l; 73tl; James Cross/Cross Sections
37; Photothèque E.D.F./M. Brigaud 81; Robert Estall
Photographs 83; Feature-Pix 21; Robert Harding
Picture Library 78; Hawaii Tribune-Herald/L.
Kadooka 43; Alan Hutchison Library 28, 50; The
Institute of Geological Sciences (N.E.R.C. copyright)
10, 27bl; Keystone Press Agency Limited 90; Klein
Associates Inc/Science Photo Library 13r; Frank
W. Lane/L. Lee Rue 75bl; The Marine Resources
Company 92; The National Maritime Museum,
London 44; National Oceanographic Atmospheric
Administration 88/9; The National Space Science
Data Center 47; Oxford Scientific Films 3, 27t, 38, 56
(P. Parks), 61, (Animals Animals/Margot Conte) 65tl
(Aqua-visuals Pty) 73br; Popperfoto 9, 31, 89; RTZ
Services Library 84b; Seaphot 18 (F. Schulke);
Science Museum, London 80, 86; Space Frontiers
Limited 6, 51, 71; The Steetley Company Limited 77;
Marie Tharp 48; Westminster Dredging Company
85; ZEFA 22/3, 66.

Front jacket photograph: Tony Stone Associates

Back jacket photograph: Oxford Scientific Films
(Laurence Gould)

Artwork by: Ray Burrows 79, 85; Kai Choi 13, 29b;
Keith Duran 36; Vana Haggerty 57, 62, 63, 64;
Ingrid Jacob 59, 60t, 60/1, 78; Ray Martin 7, 11, 17b,
21, 26, 29t, 32, 46, 49t, 69, 70, 71, 91; Carol
McCleeve 14/15; Michael Robinson 28, 30/1, 35,
41, 45, 49b, 66/7, 72/3, 87, 89; James Roper 17t, 19,
20, 23, 34, 39, 42/3; Pandora Sellars 54/5, 58;
Ed Stewart 33.

Bibliography

The Earth and Its Oceans, A. C. Duxbury;
   Addison-Wesley 1971
The Health of the Oceans, E. D. Goldberg;
   UNESCO Press 1976
Impingement of Man on the Oceans, D. Hood
   (ed.); Wiley-Interscience 1971
Introduction to Oceanography (2nd edn.),
   D. A. Ross; Prentice-Hall 1977
Introduction to Physical and Biological
   Oceanography, C. A. M. King; Edward
   Arnold 1975
Introductory Oceanography, J. Weisberg and
   H. Parish; McGraw-Hill 1974
Man and the Ocean, B. J. Skinner and K. K.
   Turekian; Prentice-Hall 1973
Oceanography, An Introduction to the Marine
   Environment, O. K. Weyl; John Wiley 1970
Oceanography, A View of the Earth, M. Grant
   Gross; Prentice-Hall 1972
Oceans (2nd edn.), K. K. Turekian; Prentice-
   Hall 1976
Ocean Science, H. W. Menard; W. H. Freeman
   1977
Principles of Oceanography (2nd edn.), R. A.
   Davis Jr.; Addison-Wesley 1977
The World Ocean: Introduction to
   Oceanography, W. A. Anikouchine and
   R. W. Sternberg; Prentice-Hall 1973